Blended Finance & Social Enterprises

Blended Finance & Social Enterprises

Addressing Risks and Impact for Healthcare Social Enterprises in India

Gautam Chakraborty

EXCELLER BOOKS®
A GLOBAL PRESS

Blended Finance &
Social Enterprises

Addressing Risks and Impact for
Healthcare Social Enterprises in India

Cover by Exceller Books

ISBN: 978-93-47397-69-1

First published in India in 2025 by Exceller Books,
An imprint of GE Group
Address: G1, Dream Apartment, Degree College Road, Belgharia,
Kolkata, 700056, India
www.excellerbooks.com

EXCELLER BOOKS®
A GLOBAL PRESS

Dedicated to

Late Dr. Barun Kanjilal, who had mentored and inspired me for the last 30 years to creatively use economics and finance as a tool to improve the lives of common folks and the needy in India and the world.

Acknowledgements

I would like to express my sincere gratitude to the following individuals and organizations for their support and guidance throughout my doctoral program.

First and foremost, I am thankful to the Swiss School of Business and Management Geneva and UpGrad for providing me with the opportunity to pursue my doctoral program online, at my own pace, without affecting my current job responsibilities. I also appreciate the six-month extension provided to me for finishing my doctoral dissertation, which allowed me to complete my research without undue stress.

I am deeply grateful to my dissertation supervisor, Dr. Ljiljana Kukec, for her guidance and encouragement throughout the doctoral program. Her expertise and support were invaluable to me, and I appreciate the time she took to review my work and provide feedback.

I would also like to thank Mr. Himanshu Sikka, who leads the SAMRIDH blended finance initiative, for introducing me to the social enterprises supported by SAMRIDH. Furthermore, I would like to express my appreciation to the social entrepreneurs, who cannot be named for ethical considerations, who shared their time and expertise with me, providing me with valuable information and insights that enriched my research. I am grateful for their willingness to open up about their experiences and share their knowledge with me. This opportunity allowed me to gain valuable insights and collect data that was essential to my research.

I would also like to thank my colleagues, Dr. Neeta Rao, Ms. Kachina Chawla, and Dr. Subrato Mondal, for their continuous support and encouragement throughout my journey in this program. Their advice and feedback were invaluable to me, and I appreciate the time they took to review my work and provide suggestions.

Finally, I would like to thank my wife, Ms. Sumana Banerjee, for her moral, material, and personal support throughout my doctoral program. Her encouragement and patience were essential to my success, and I am grateful for her love and support.

Abstract

It is increasingly seen that the investments required for sustainable development cannot be met by the public or private entities on their own. The challenge is looking for ways that can bring together the private investments along with public funds through blended financing. There are very few blended finance platforms for supporting healthcare social enterprises, especially in countries like India. Hence, this research aims to study the risks faced by healthcare social enterprises and how blended finance can address those risks in the Indian healthcare context. The research uses a qualitative case-study method and conceptual modeling, using grounded theory and framework analysis. Four case studies were developed covering different healthcare social enterprises that have adopted blended finance to de-risk their operations and accelerate healthcare social impact in India. The social enterprises were selected for the case studies from a limited universe of such enterprises in India adopting blended finance. Data collection involved In-Depth Interview (IDI) of the healthcare social entrepreneurs and review of project documents, websites and other such information shared by the entrepreneurs. The study shows that social enterprises address social impact, business risks, financial risks, and business viability through innovative approaches that go beyond traditional understanding. The case studies hint at the importance of context in shaping social enterprise strategies, the crucial role of technology in enabling scale and efficiency, the significance of partnerships in risk management and the innovation in financial models, particularly blended finance. The study demonstrates that successful healthcare social enterprises combine innovative business models, strategic use of blended finance, strong focus on accessibility and affordability, effective use of technology and strategic partnerships. The study also indicates that blended finance mitigates the risks faced by social enterprises through financial risk reduction, operational risk management, and market risk mitigation. In addition, the study shows that blended finance helps social enterprises address social impact by improving access, enhancing quality, achieving scale, and supporting innovation. This is captured in a suggested conceptual model of how blended finance enables social enterprises to address risks and impact, which can guide global investors looking to invest in social enterprises.

Table of Contents

List of Tables

List of Figures

Chapter 1 | Introduction

1.1. Introduction

Social goods had traditionally been the domain of the government, relying on public finances. But increasingly, it is seen that the investments required for sustainable development, involving social goods – balancing economic, social, and environmental progress – are huge and cannot be met by public or private entities on their own. The challenge is to find ways and means to bring together private investments and public funds working in the social sector. This is where the social enterprises play an important role, operating at the junction of the commercial and social sectors.

There is a research gap in a comprehensive blended financing framework to evaluate commercial, philanthropic, and public investments in social enterprises (SEs). Also, there is a lack of sufficient research to determine whether the role of philanthropic and public funds in healthcare SEs is limited to de-risking commercial investments or whether they play other roles as well.

1.2. Research Problem

This research focuses on the hybrid approach of combining public and private resources for social good – broadly termed blended financing, mentioned first in the Addis Ababa Action Agenda for the Third International Conference on Financing for Development (2015). Blended finance has been emerging as a unique way of mobilizing private resources for social good, by using public resources to catalyze these private funds. But there are very few blended finance platforms for supporting healthcare social enterprises, especially in countries like India. Hence, we do not yet have a good understanding of how such blended structures are able to address the business and financial risks faced by the healthcare social enterprises.

1.3. Purpose of Research

The primary purpose of the research is to develop a conceptual model of blended financing of social enterprises, especially in the context of the health sector in India. Particularly, the study has the following sub-objectives:

- Explore the financing challenges faced by the healthcare social enterprises in India and the financial and advisory support they need to sustain and expand their healthcare enterprises, while achieving social and health impact.
- Study the implications of mixing different types of capital through blended financing on the business and financial risk of the healthcare social enterprises in India and on the social and health impact achieved by such enterprises.

1.4. Significance of the Study

Martin (2015), in his article on hybrid financing for impact businesses, views social enterprises as phenomena that combine resources in novel ways to produce social value. This study focuses on a hybrid approach that combines public and private resources for social good. Blended financing, a term in vogue since mentioned in the Addis Ababa Action Agenda for the Third International Conference on Financing for Development (2015), has been emerging as a unique way of mobilizing private resources for social good, by using public resources to catalyze these private funds. But there are very few blended finance platforms for supporting healthcare social enterprises, especially in countries like India. Hence, we do not yet have a clear understanding of whether such blended structures can address the business and financial risks faced by healthcare social enterprises, especially those looking to grow beyond the "proof-of-concept" stage. As per the primer on blended finance by Organization of Economic Co-operation and Development (OECD) in 2015, enterprises that grow out of the "Explore" stage and gets into the "Build" and "Grow" stages and are no longer burdened with the feasibility risk, but start experiencing business model risk, are faced with funding shortfall and small deal-size issues, but are not yet looking at liquidity, refinancing, or exit. Such enterprises leave behind the need for pure grant funding and look for blended finance options like repayable grants, junior equity, and flexible debts.

This study explores how blended finance options work for different types of healthcare social enterprises in India, each at a different stage of business growth. In addition, this study explores whether social enterprises need more than just financing to scale up and sustain their social impact. As global capital flows target sustainable economic and development impact and seek new investment opportunities in social enterprises, the findings of this study are expected to help investors and social enterprises in hitherto neglected sectors like healthcare make informed investment decisions to scale social impact economically.

1.5. Research Purpose and Questions

Given the shortage of research on healthcare social enterprises and their use of blended finance for growth, this research aims to study the risks faced by healthcare social enterprises and how blended finance can address those risks in the Indian healthcare context. Given that blended finance, especially in the healthcare sector, is at a nascent stage in India and globally, the study develops a conceptual framework of risk, returns, and impact for healthcare social enterprises, employing a grounded theory approach.

Because of grounded theory, the research does not start with any explicit hypothesis but has the following broad research questions.

- How do social enterprises address social impact and business viability?

- What are the risks of healthcare social enterprises in India?
- How does the mixing of commercial investments and donor grants in blended financing structures enable healthcare social enterprises to address risks and achieve social impact?

Chapter 2 | Review of Literature

2.1. Theoretical Framework

This research aims to understand the role of blended finance in addressing the risks faced by social enterprises – both financial and business risks - in the healthcare sector. In addition, the role of social enterprises in addressing social impact and sustainability is also analyzed, along with the role of blended finance in it. This calls for reviewing the concepts of sustainable development and impact, social enterprises and blended finance. Also, apart from the concepts, it is also important to know current gaps in understanding the role blended finance plays in enabling social enterprises to address risks and accelerate social impact, especially in the health sector.

Hence, the review of literature covers the concepts, existing knowledge, and any gaps, if any, in sustainable development, social enterprises, and blended finance. These are discussed in the subsequent sections, ending with identifying the research gaps.

Given the focus on sustainable development, social enterprises and blended finance, all publicly available literature on this topic was covered in the review. The types of literature reviewed included journal articles, books, monographs, working papers, reports, and conference proceedings.

The literature review on sustainable development covered a broad conceptual treatment and the history of how those concepts evolved from environmental sustainability and the triple bottom line to the Millennium Development Goals and Sustainable Development Goals. The concept of environment, social, and governance (ESG) lensed investments is also covered. Here, the focus was only on the concepts and their evolution, not on identifying knowledge gaps. This is more to provide context for the actual focus of this research.

The literature on social enterprises included a search for understanding their nature, characteristics, and how they balance social impact with economic viability. Existing knowledge and the current knowledge gap with special reference to healthcare social enterprises were also covered in the literature search.

The research on blended finance aimed to trace its evolution, examine its application to social enterprises, especially in the health sector, and identify current knowledge gaps. The literature on social enterprises, the health sector, and developing countries/the global south was also explored.

The emerging framework of sustainable development and social enterprises, while considering investors and philanthropic/public funders through a possible blended finance arrangement, is synthesized in figure 2.1 below.

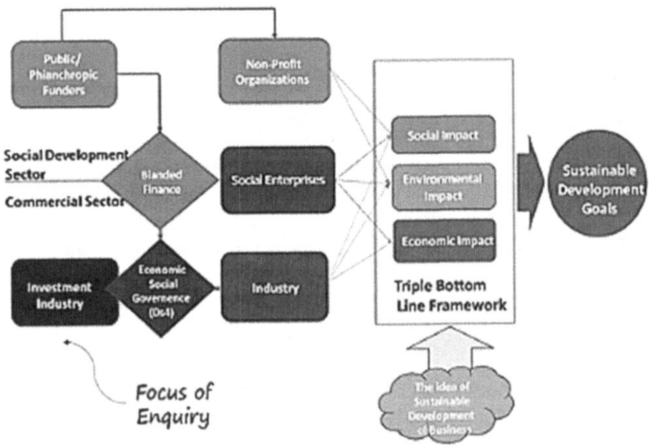

Figure 2.1: Framework of Sustainable Development Affect Linking Social Enterprises and Financing

As per the framework presented above, industries focus primarily on economic impact, with social and environmental impact being an additionality to their economic activity; non-profits focus primarily on social and/or environmental impact, with economic impact being an additionality. It is only the social enterprises that focus on all three aspects of the triple bottom line as their primary focus. Also, social enterprises get blended funding, which is a mix of commercial investment and philanthropic/public funding, whereas industries get commercial investments, which is showing an ESG lens of investing lately. On the other hand, non-profits receive only philanthropic and public funding, with no commercial investments, as their activities are essentially non-commercial. The focus of enquiry in this research is depicted by the red dotted triangle, which covers commercial investors, social enterprises, and public/philanthropic funders, and includes ESG investing as well as blended finance arrangements.

2.2. Theory of Sustainable Development, Triple Bottom Line and ESG Investing

The idea of sustainable development, which arose from concern about the degradation of the natural environment caused by industrial activities, has slowly gained momentum as a definition of "good" business behavior and is seen as desirable to ensure businesses do not make the world "unlivable". As per Duran et al (2015), "sustainable development has become a recognized goal for human society since the deterioration of environmental conditions in many parts of the world" (Bossel, 1999). Hence, increasing attention is given to the environment. The importance of environmental impact is rising as industrialization is placing a greater burden on the environment (Wall & Gong, 2001).

Duran et al. go on to explain that "sustainable development" signifies two elements: "sustainability," which represents durability, and "development," which aims to expand or construct potentialities, gradually bringing them to a fuller, greater, or better state. The role of sustainable development in society has been recognized since 1992, at the Earth Summit in Rio de Janeiro, and has been reiterated at the World Summit on Sustainable Development in Johannesburg in 2002. In this emerging paradigm of "sustainable development", it is not just about environmental protection, but it also "connects other areas, especially those involving economic activity" (Krajnc & Glavic, 2005).

The ecological aspect of sustainable development relates not only to economic development but also to the entire gamut of development. Environmental protection is the stability of the physical and biological systems and their capacity to adapt to change (Bran, 1991). The understanding is that economic growth should not affect the environment.

In contrast to environmental sustainability, the concept of social sustainability involves "social interactions, relationships, behavioral patterns, and values of humanity" (Dempsey et al., 2011).

As per Frant and Minica (Frant & Minica, 2008), the human aspect of sustainable development worldwide involves the following:

- Promotion of education, training and public support for the environment
- Protecting and promoting human health (focused on access to medical facilities, especially in rural areas, control of infectious diseases, risks of pollution and ecological risk).
- Fight against poverty (through access of the poor to sustainable livelihoods, promoting human development and integrated policy investment in human capital).
- Demographic trends threatening sustainable development (especially population growth in developing countries).

As per Keiner (Keiner, 2005), "the idea of 'sustainable development' was born in 1713 when Carlowitz edited the first book on forest sciences" who said that "we should organize our economy in a way that we will not suffer scarcity [of timber], and where it is lumbered, we should strive for young growth at its place". Carlowitz's emphasis on the ongoing use of resources is central to the concept of sustainable development, which found its way into the political vision in 1987 by the World Commission on Environment and Development (also known as the Brundtland Commission; WCED, 1987).

The Swiss 'Monitoring of Sustainable Development Project' (MONET) modified the definition given in the Brundtland Commission report, using "key elements like justice, intra- and inter-generational equity, maintenance of options, meeting of needs, and maintenance of biodiversity". As a result, MONET defines sustainable development as "Sustainable development means ensuring dignified living conditions regarding human rights by creating and maintaining the widest possible range of options for freely defining life plans. The principle of fairness among and between present and future generations should be considered in the use of environmental, economic, and social resources. Putting these needs into practice entails comprehensive protection of biodiversity in terms of ecosystem, species, and genetic diversity, all of which are the vital foundations of life."

The popular model of sustainability involves the triangle of environmental (conservation), economic (growth), and social (equity) dimensions (see figure 2.2 below).

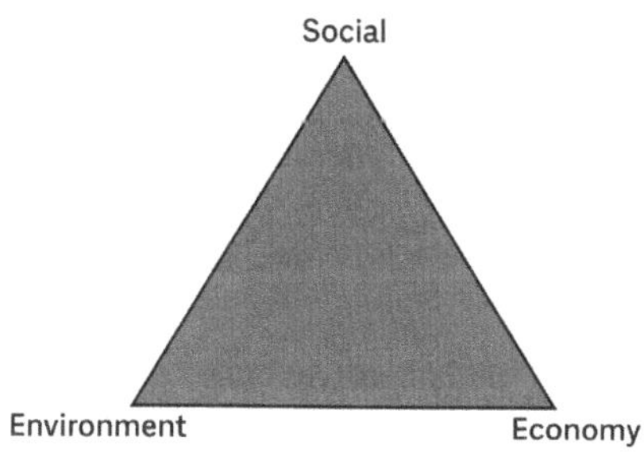

Figure 2.2: The Three Pillar (Triangle) Basic Model Of Sustainability, Sometimes Shown As Three Interlocking Circles
Source: Keiner, 2005

In 1994, a study group of the World Bank developed the "capital stock model" as given below.

Capital stock of Sustainable Development (CSD)	= Σ	Capital stock of the Environment (CEn) + Capital stock of the Economy (CEc) + Capital stock of the Society (CS)

Here, the environmental capital stock includes biodiversity, landscape, mineral resources, clean air, and clean water. The social capital stock relates to health, social security, social cohesion, freedom, justice, equality of opportunity, and peace.

Alternative models to the "triangle of sustainability" have emerged lately. There is the "prism of sustainable development" model (Spangenberg & Bonniot, 1998), as depicted in figure 2.3, that includes the following four dimensions:

- Economic dimension (man-made capital)
- Environmental dimension (natural capital), and
- Social dimension (human capital), as the base for
- Institutional dimension (social capital)

There are indicators to measure how far one has come in comparison to the overall vision of sustainable development (Valentin & Spangenberg, 1999).

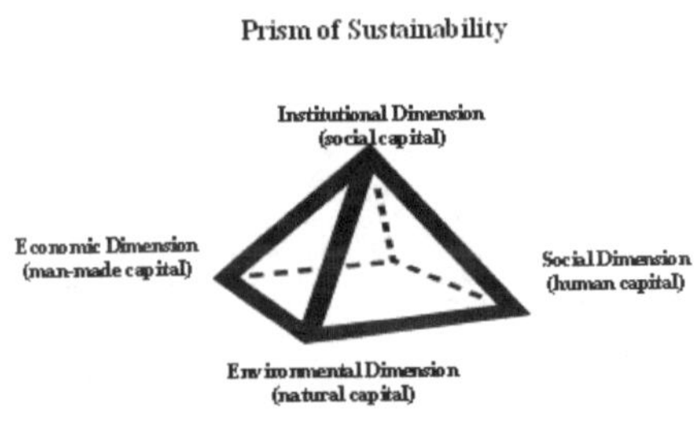

Figure 2.3: The Prism of Sustainable Development
Source: Stenberg 2001, P. 42

As per Keiner, "the economic dimension tends to include assets emanating from all four dimensions, thus, adding confusion to the description and analysis". Consequently, he proposed "MAIN prism of sustainable development", as shown in figure 2.4 below. This model used the terms of Mind, Artefact, Institution and Nature to "relieve the prism from the burden of expressions as social and economic", which felt more confusing.

MAIN Prism of Sustainability

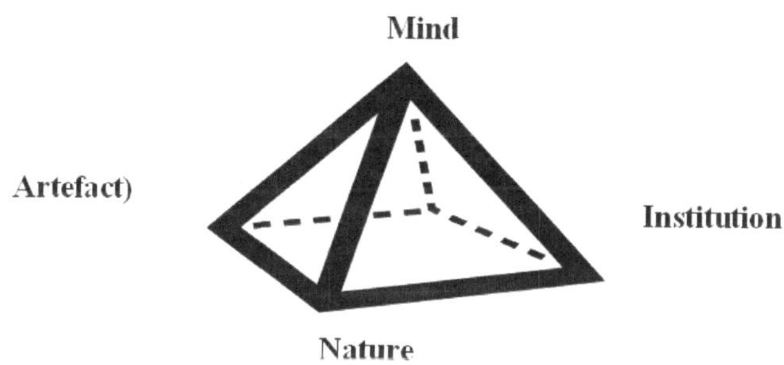

Figure 2.4: The MAIN Prism of Sustainable Development
Source: Stenberg 2001, P. 43

The environmental dimension (nature) comprises natural capital, which is further categorized into stocks of non-renewable and renewable resources. The economic dimension (artefact) represents all man-made assets such as buildings and roads. The social dimension (mind) is conceptualized as the awareness of the individual, including their worldview, knowledge, and experience. The institutional dimension is how society is organized and the relations between people. The criticism of the prism models is that they pay too much attention to human and institutional capital and neglect the natural capital.

The International Development Research Centre proposes to replace the PRIMs models with the 'Egg of Sustainability' model, as shown in Figure 2.5. This was conceptualized by the International

Union for the Conservation of Nature (IUCN) in 1994, as shown in figure 2.5 below (Guijt & Moiseev, 2001).

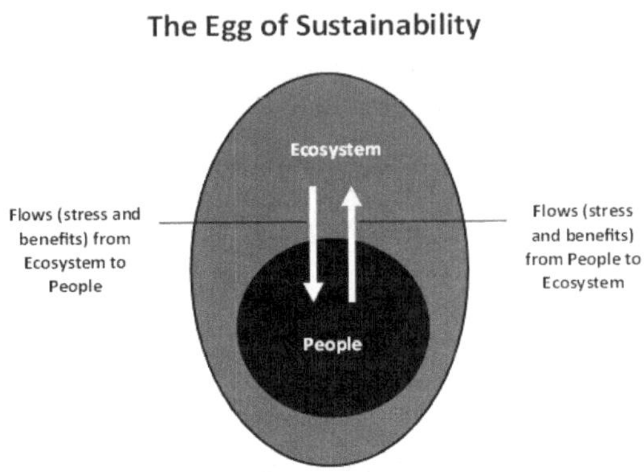

Figure 2.5: IUCN's Egg of Sustainability
Source: IUCN 1994

The 'Egg of Sustainability' depicts people within the ecosystem, and both are dependent on each other. Also, "just as an egg is good only if both the white and yolk are good, so a society is well and sustainable only if both the people and the ecosystem are well" (Guijt & Moiseev, 2001). It means that social and economic well-being occurs only if the environment ensures the provision of raw materials, space for new production sites and jobs, and qualities like recreation and health.

As per Alhaddi, "some studies used sustainability to primarily refer to the environmental line. Others used the term to refer to the social line, while some used the term to refer to all three." In this context, the Triple Bottom Line (TBL) places equal importance on each of the three lines, thereby bringing a semblance of balance and coherence. TBL was coined by Elkington (1997) as a concept related to sustainability. As per Goel, "Driven by sustainability, TBL provides a framework for measuring the performance of the business and the success of the organization using three lines: economic, social, and environmental" (Goel, 2010).

In essence, TBL expresses the expansion of the environmental agenda in a way that integrates the economic and social lines (Elkington, 1997). In his definition of TBL, Elkington used the terms profit, people, and the planet as the three lines. The economic line ties the growth of the organization to the growth of the economy and how well it contributes to support it. In other words, it focuses on the economic value provided by the organization to the surrounding system, in a way that benefits it and promotes its capacity to support future generations. The social performance focuses on the interaction between the community and the organization and addresses issues of community involvement, employee relations, and fair wages (Goel, 2010). Like the social aspect of TBL, environmental initiatives affect the business sustainability of organizations. The environmental line of TBL refers to engaging in practices that do not compromise the environmental resources for future generations.

As per Alhaddi, "unlike sustainability, there is considerably less empirical research on TBL" (Alhaddi, 2015). The limited literature available has focused more on the accounting and finance aspects. Alhaddi further mentions that Elkington, the proponent of the term 'TBL', "now recognizes the paradigm as a failure, since the capitalist system was unsuccessful in giving more space to the social and environmental spheres over the economic one". Elkington feels that, despite emerging frameworks for the triple bottom line, it still does not consistently generate positive returns across all three aspects (Elkington, 2018). Although the practice of TBL has generated various measures and indices, such as the Global Reporting Initiative, Dow Jones Sustainability Indices, Full Cost Accounting, and BCG's Total Societal Impact, it has led to significant confusion and heterogeneity (Beal et al., 2017).

In the 25 years since Elkington introduced TBL, the framework has also been associated with other aspects of the sustainable supply chain. On the other hand, Gladwin, Kennelly, and Krause relate TBL to risk management as businesses must "consider threats caused by harmful destructions like climate change, resource scarcity and insecurities, population growth, and all concepts related to the security and maintenance of the business" (Gladwin, Kennelly, and Krause, 1995).

Montabon, Pagell, and Wu suggest "the need for a new paradigm shift toward a holistic framework that encompasses the triple bottom line as the main paradigm for sustainable development" (Montabon, Pagell, and Wu, 2016). As Milne and Gray suggested, "TBL can also be designed as a direction to take and consider a double bottom line as a starting point toward the aim of a sustainable development, which has the possibility to be reached through the adoption of an integrating framework, since TBL by itself is considered an insufficient instrument to reach financial, social, and economic sustainability" (Milne & Gray, 2013).

Svensson et al. suggest adding aspects of stakeholder integration, transparency, and strategic and cultural change to future research on operations management and sustainability. This would need to "involve quantitative methods, investigating how these capabilities can be implemented in the framework successfully, with the subsequent result of a theory building that finally considers all TBL dimensions" (Svensson et al., 2016). Eskandarpour et al. also suggested including the social bottom line in the equation (Eskandarpour et al., 2015).

Svensson et al. conducted two literature reviews on the triple bottom line approach in 2016 and 2018 (Svensson et al., 2016, 2018). They noticed a "strong association between the TBL and other business sustainability efforts involving either one or two of the bottom lines".

Winter and Knemeyer (2013) noted in their literature review that the concept of TBL "has gained suggestive preeminence in research, but it is also worrisome how the term has been used controversially to denote only the economic and either the social or the environmental bottom line, despite Elkington holistic-based idea". Also, Walker, et al, found from their review that "the majority of sustainable supply chain management research from 2002 to 2014 did not mention the social bottom line" while focusing exclusively on economic and environmental bottom lines (Walker, et al, 2014).

However, despite this confusion, TBL has been gaining credibility over the years, as evidenced by an increase in publications from 2015 to 2019 in both databases, as shown in figure 2.6 below (Loviscek, 2021).

As per Schleich, "based on the TBL concept, a new encompassing framework was created to measure performance beyond the traditional accounting standards of return on investment and shareholder financial value" (Schleich, 2021). This new encompassing framework morphed into the "Environmental, Social and Governance" (ESG) framework, with the United Nations Secretary General, Kofi Annan, inviting Chief Executive Officers (CEOs) from leading financial institutions globally, to join an initiative of building stronger and resilient financial markets through sustainable development. The Secretary General's letter included a report by Ivo Knoepfel, who coined the term 'ESG' for Environmental, Social, and Governance aspects (The Global Compact, 2004). Lokuwaduge notes that, since the letter written by the Secretary General was on 'ESG', "addressing environmental, social and governance matters has gradually become a critical component of business strategy" (Lokuwaduge, 2016). Lokuwaduge further says that "although the ESG concept is generally more related to financial markets and investors, stakeholder engagement is usually crucial to enhance companies' environmental policies, as well as global sustainable development".

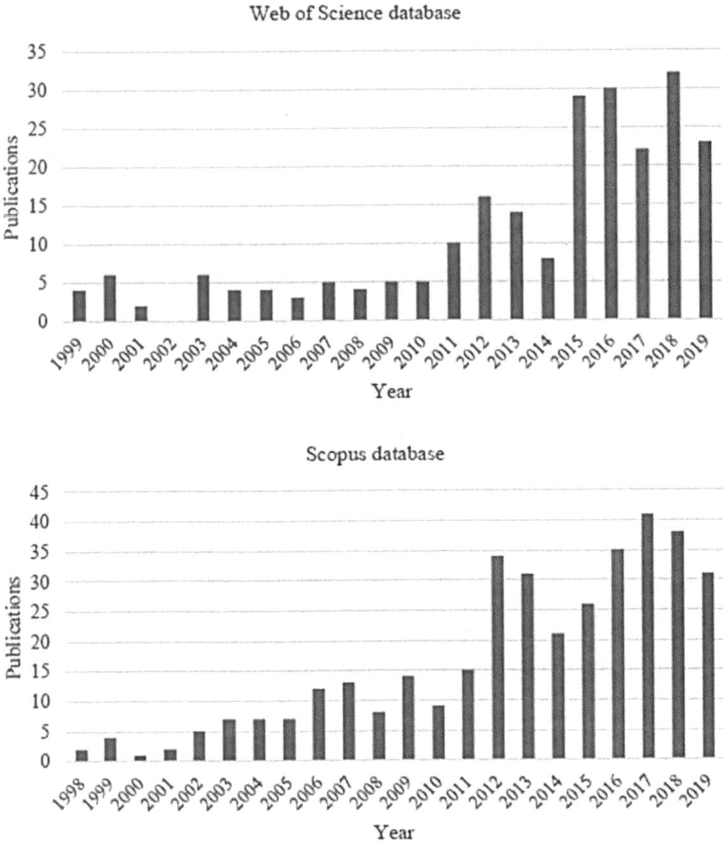

Figure 2.6: Frequency of Triple Bottom Line in Publications by Year
Source: Loviscek, 2021

Armstrong observes that the "term ESG has become fundamentally a financial market concept" (Armstrong, 2020). The integration of ESG metrics into investment portfolios is now an industry norm (Bertolotti, 2020). Foubert estimates that the assets under management (AUM) of Funds adopting an ESG investment lens have grown to over $40 trillion, from $30 trillion in 2018 and $22 trillion in 2016 (Foubert, 2020).

As per Ho and Park, by 2019, "more than 85% of the SandP 500 participants in the United States and more than 90% of the largest global firms produce sustainability reports with some sort of ESG information disclosure; many organizations also voluntarily include sustainability or other ESG items in their annual reports" (Ho & Park, 2019). Schleich notes that ESG metrics might have seemed like a paradigm that could hold the investor community's interest only for a short time before being replaced by newer ideas, but the Coronavirus pandemic seems to have renewed investors' interest and demand for sustainable products. This was evident from increased resources inflow into ESG funds in the first quarter of 2020 in the United States, with commensurate outflows from non-ESG segments (Schleich, 2021).

Mervelskemper and Streit have concluded that "ESG practices seem to indeed generate stronger value to adopting firms" (Mervelskemper & Streit, 2017). Lopez-de-Silanes et al. found that disclosure of "ESG information is correlated to decreased risk perception" after analyzing business entities in the United States, the United Kingdom, Japan, Switzerland, Australia, and France (Lopez-de-Silanes et al., 2020). In the post-COVID-19 pandemic era, Broadstock et al. found that Chinese companies with stronger ESG standards outperformed those with weaker ESG standards. Broadstock also found that "ESG performance mitigates financial risks during a financial crisis" (Broadstock et al., 2021).

On the other hand, there is literature claiming the contrary. Fatemi, et al, have stated that "ESG disclosure, per se, seems to decrease firms' valuation, whereas others have suggested that Companies that were not part of International Securities Exchange (ISE) presented better financial performance" (Fatemi, et al, 2018). In this regard, Dalal and Thaker feel that "ESG reporting, indexation and related performance is still a subject in its infancy. Therefore, the lack of standardization across so many indicators, dimensions, information suppliers and platforms, together with different frameworks for sundry stakeholders, might distort results" (Dalal & Thaker, 2019).

As far as countries like India are concerned, Ghosh and Rajan mention that "there is a need for active participation of businesses to turn sustainable development challenges into opportunities and play a key role in meeting Sustainable Development Goals (SDGs) targets" (Ghosh & Rajan, 2019). An analysis of the SDGs and Indian industries by Singh and Rahman shows that companies in the industrial segments of cement, construction, fertilizers and pesticides, industrial manufacturing, power, and telecom had adopted the SDGs (Singh & Rahman, 2021). They further found that fewer than half of the companies in the chemicals, financial services, pharma, and services industries have adopted the SDGs. In terms of adopting social SDGs, which include health (SDG-3), the analysis shows that firms working in industries such as oil and gas, financial services, cement, consumer goods are more concerned about it, while companies in chemicals, fertilizers, industrial manufacturing, services, pharma, power, and telecom sectors are concerned with SDG-3. Overall, among the top 100 Indian companies, SDG-8 (Decent work and economic growth) was found to be given top priority, followed by SDG-3 (Good health and well-being), SDG-4 (Quality education), and SDG-5 (Gender equality). Williams stated that "embedding SDGs into key business processes has a long-term commercial significance. Businesses should align their key processes with the SDGs to find new growth opportunities and reduce the risk associated with their profiles" (Williams, 2015). Scheyvens et al. also conclude that the "achievement of SDGs depends on the speed with which companies develop more innovative and inclusive business models" (Scheyvens et al., 2016).

Singh and Rahman conclude that "in future exploration, researchers should perform studies in the same industry segment, and in different countries, for a better understanding of SDGs adoption" (Singh & Rahman, 2021).

2.3. Social Enterprises and generating Sustainable Development Outcomes

Coming to social businesses, also referred to as social enterprises, these are increasingly seen as drivers of economic growth and development by adopting the rules of business enterprises and blending them to create social, economic, and environmental value. By blending the social, economic, and environmental values in their businesses, social enterprises become key players in ensuring sustainable development.

Terziev and Arabska say that "social entrepreneurship actively involves the fulfilment of social objectives by promoting sustainable development and thereby meeting the sustainable development goals" (Terziev & Arabska, 2017). Macassa emphasizes the important role social enterprises play "in helping to address the complex societal challenges included in the SDG agenda" (Macassa, 2021).

Zhang and Swanson postulate that social enterprises (SEs) help respond to societal challenges in two ways. Firstly, through the development or adoption of a solution (social innovation). Secondly, by making sure that the solution is accessible (scaling the social innovation) based on a viable business model (Zhang & Swanson, 2014).

Others, like Stratan, have argued that "SEs can deliver social impact through business models that use principles of circular economy, with a focus on social and environmental problems, contributing to cost saving, new forms of revenue, resource conservation, and long-term competitiveness, as well as driving for sustainable development" (Stratan, 2017). Holt and Littlewood suggest that SEs can "contribute to SDGs by generating positive social and environmental impacts at the input stage by ethical sourcing of products." An SE can "also employ individuals from marginalized populations, or generate a positive social impact through the products and services they offer, or through direct programs and interventions" (Holt & Littlewood, 2015).

Seelos and Mair feel that social entrepreneurship can stimulate ideas for more socially acceptable and sustainable business strategies by encouraging established companies to take on greater social responsibility (Seelos & Mair, 2005). Leadbeater finds that "social entrepreneurs innovate new solutions to chronic social problems that are more efficient than the public sector and activate a virtuous circle of social capital within local communities" (Leadbeater, 1997). Scaling up of these innovative solutions, "can bring us a step closer to the objectives of the Sustainable Development Agenda" (Rahdari et al, 2016).

The term social entrepreneurs or social entrepreneurship was first used by Bowen in 1953 in the book titled "Social Responsibilities of the Businessman" (Bowen, 1953). Later, Joseph Banks, in the work titled "The Sociology of Social Movements", described social entrepreneurs as "those who trace the need of using managerial skills to address business and social challenges" (Banks, 1972). The concept of the social enterprise became more prominent in the 1990s, "spawning from discussions highlighting cooperativism regarding the Social Economy and business schools that were touting initiatives for social change" (Nyssens, 2006). Nyssens describes social enterprises as businesses situated within the context of a social economy "whose main criteria is to benefit the community by reinvesting surplus for the purpose of the community. It differs from other forms of more traditional organization models in the sense that its primary motivation is not controlled by generating more profit. There is a small amount of paid work and a decent amount of economic risk that comes with the autonomy of a Social Enterprise" (Nyssens, 2006).

Sealey, et al, find that "non-profit organizations have long engaged in income generation and businesses to either supplement or complement their mission activities" (Sealey, et al, 2000). Kim Alter found that, "beginning in the 1960s, US non-profits experimented with enterprises to create jobs for disadvantaged populations. Micro-credit organizations made their appearance in developing countries by the 1970s, at about the same time Community Development Corporations (CDCs) were gaining popularity in the United States.

However, it is only in the last 15 or 20 years that academics, practitioners, and donors have been studying and recording cases of non-profits adopting market-based approaches to achieve their missions" (Alter, 2007).

The Roberts Foundation Homeless Economic Development Fund defined social enterprise as "a revenue-generating venture founded to create economic opportunities for very low-income individuals, while simultaneously operating with reference to the financial bottom-line." (Emerson & Twersky, 1996). This definition captures the social and financial characteristics of the social enterprise, emphasizing social enterprise as a program approach.

According to Kim Alter, "Social Enterprise" and "Socially Responsible Business", forming the middle of the hybrid spectrum, serve dual objectives. The first is the Social Objective, aimed at mission A (social value creation), which varies widely depending on the organization's mission and sector. The second one is Financial Objectives focused on financial sustainability (economic value creation), which varies according to funding needs and business model, where financial measures are drawn from both private and non-profit practice."

Kim Alter describes the spectrum of practitioners from purely philanthropic organizations to purely commercial organizations, with the hybrid forms in the middle (representing the social enterprises), as shown in table 2.1 below.

	Purely Philanthropic	**Hybrid (Social Enterprises)**	**Purely Commercial**
Motives	Appeal to goodwill	Mixed motives	Appeal to self-interest
Methods	Mission-driven	Balance of mission and market	Market-driven
Goals	Social value creation	Social and economic value creation	Economic value creation

Destination of Income/Profit	Directed toward mission activities of nonprofit organization (required by law or organizational policy)	Reinvested in mission activities or operational expenses, and/or retained for business growth (for-profits may redistribute a portion)	Distributed to shareholders and owners

Table 2.1: Spectrum of Practitioners
Source: Alter, 2007

Alter further classifies the social enterprises based on their respective operating models, as shown in table 2.2 below.

Social Enterprise Models	Value Proposition	Mission	Financial Sustainability
1. Entrepreneur Support Model	Sell business support and financial services to its target population or firms. Social enterprise clients then sell their products and services in the open market.	Facilitate the financial security of its clients by supporting their entrepreneurial activities	Through the sales of its services to clients, income is used to cover costs associated with delivering entrepreneur support services as well as the business' operating expenses
2. Market Intermediary Model	Provide services to its target population or small producers (individuals, firm or cooperatives), to help them access markets. The market intermediary either purchases the client-made products outright or takes them on consignment and	Strengthen markets and facilitating clients' financial security by helping them develop and sell their products	Through the sale of its client-made products, income is used to pay the business' operating expenses and to cover program costs of rendering product development, marketing, and credit services to clients

	then sells the products in high margin markets at a mark-up.		
3. Employment Model	Provides employment opportunities and job training to its target populations or people with high barriers to employment such as disabled, homeless, at-risk youth, and ex-offenders	Create employment opportunities for clients	Through the sales of its products and services, income is used to pay standard operating expenses associated with the business and additional social costs incurred by employing its clients
4. Fee-for-Service Model	Commercializes its social services, and then sells them directly to the target populations, such as individuals, firms, communities, or to a third-party payer	Render social services in the sector it works in, such as health or education	Through fees charged for services
5. Low-Income Client as Market Model	Provide poor and low-income clients access to products and services whereby price, distribution, product features, etc. bar access for this market	Provide access to necessary goods and services to the poor	Must rely on developing creative distribution systems, lowering production and marketing costs, achieving high operating efficiencies, cross subsidizing creative revenue markets to markets that require subsidy
6. Cooperative Model	Provide direct benefit to its target population, such as cooperative members, through	Providing members services	Through the sales of its products and services to its members (clients) as well as in

	member services: market information, technical assistance/extension services, collective bargaining power, economies of bulk purchase, access to products and services, access to external markets for member-produced products and services, etc.		commercial markets
7. Market Linkage (Market Aggregator) Model	Functions as a broker connecting buyers to producers and vice versa and charging fees for this service	Linking markets	Income generated from enterprise activities
8. Service Subsidization Model	Sells products or services to an external market and uses the income to fund its social programs. The business mandate is separate from its social mission.	Social mission subsidized by profits from separate business	Business profits

Table 2.2: Classification of Social Enterprises
Source: Alter, 2007

Massarsky found that the non-profits also engage in business activities to enhance revenue for their core social mission (Massarsky, 2006). However, Massarsky discovered that "an overwhelming percentage of social enterprise organizations (71%) are unprofitable and many fail within their first five years." Research by Bradach and Foster revealed that "social enterprise may lead to mission drift and less service delivered to the original recipients of services" (Bradach & Foster, 2005).

Looking specifically at SDG-3 (Health), researchers like Roy, et al, Kilgore-Nolan M, and Henderson, et al, argue that "SEs can help address the social determinants of health towards the achievement of health equity, which in turn will contribute to the attainment of the SDGs and, specifically, SDG-3" (Roy, et al, 2014; Kilgore-Nolan M, 2018; Henderson, et al, 2020). Rychetnik, et al conclude that the work of SEs on health equity impacts SGD-3 outcomes through a "set of actions with a coherent objective to bring about change or produce identifiable outcomes" (Rychetnik et al, 2002).

Macassa says that the "Social" theme addressed by social enterprises includes health as a sub-sector, and that social enterprises can reduce inequalities in health (through social, economic, and/or environmental action on social determinants of health) in a variety of contexts. "Social determinants of health" are the conditions other than actual healthcare that are crucial to the attainment of good health by the people. Macassa argues that "rather than acting on individual risk factors such as smoking, alcohol, diet, and exercise (a pathogenic approach to health), SEs address inequities more broadly by acting on the social, economic, and environmental circumstances of the most vulnerable members of society" (Macassa G., 2021).

As SEs utilize and build upon existing community resources or "social assets" to promote health and well-being, they "change the conditions that lead to adverse health behaviors rather than simply focusing on their deficiencies" (Roy, et al, 2014; Gordon, et al, 2018). Borzaga and Depedri and Christoforou and Davis show that "SEs can play a significant role in building and maintaining social capital, which constituted the social networks, together with shared norms, values and understandings, that facilitate co-operation within and among groups" (Borzaga C, Depedri S., 2014; Christoforou A, Davis JB., 2014). Similarly, Drayton also states "that across the world, SEs can also alleviate poverty and provide care to the most disadvantaged groups in society, which in turn improves health, well-being, and quality of life" (Drayton, et al, 2006).

According to Macassa, there are several challenges to consider. Firstly, to date, public health professionals still need to fully embrace businesses (for-profit or not) as partners in promoting health and well-being in achieving SDG-3. Conversely, businesses (especially SEs) do not yet see public health institutions and practitioners as potential partners in their work with communities. Secondly, there is the challenge of gaining a better understanding of how, and through what activities, SEs will more effectively impact the health and well-being of individuals and communities towards the attainment of the SDGs, specifically SDG-3. Thirdly, there are those who argue that the SDGs fail to properly acknowledge the potential central role that business, in general, will need to play if they are to be achieved, and, more especially, the potential contribution of responsible trading, social entrepreneurship, and SEs. Fourthly, the role of responsible leadership within SEs needs to be better understood. This includes understanding how such leadership may impact the drive for successful change, as well as activities that might lead to sustainable population health. "Future public health research needs to include the leadership dimension in parallel with the other aspects of the relation between SEs, health and well-being that are already being researched" (Macassa G., 2021).

As Wendy Pardee notes, social enterprises require entrepreneurial qualities and emphasize earned income. "Many non-profits engage in social enterprise to improve their bottom line. With social enterprise, there is suddenly an increased focus on financial performance." This means social enterprise may need more "business" skills and a "business" focus on financial performance. However, whether social businesses can continue with a primary focus on social mission, or they need to become more "business-like, has not been answered by most of the prior or existing literature (Wendy Pardee, 2010).

2.4. Financing of Social Enterprises and Blended Finance

Bataeva has listed some international organizations and foundations that support and finance social entrepreneurship. Among them, "there are organizations in which the support of social entrepreneurship is one of the activities (like Western NIS Enterprise Fund, Renaissance, British Council) and there are those, for which the development and spread of this entrepreneurship is the main goal of the activity" (Bataeva, 2015).

According to Akbulaev et al. (2019), there are European and American models of financing social enterprises, as shown in table 2.3 below.

Criteria	American Model	European Model
Main source of funding social enterprises	Foundations, Private donations, and Revenue from sale of goods and services	Grants, Investor capital, Membership fee, Private donations, and Revenue from sale of goods and services
Goals of social business	Essentially a non-profit entity with self-financing	Essentially a business with social goals
Availability of government financial support programs	No government programs	Active government programs

Table 2.3: Comparison Between the American and European Models of Financing Social Entrepreneurship

Source: Akbulaev, Et Al, 2019

The American model relies primarily on business revenues for financing and does not rely much on special public (government) financing for social enterprises. In contrast, the European model draws mainly from the public sources of financing, and the profits from operations of the social enterprises are less significant in their financing.

As per Akbulaev et al, "in Western Europe, businessmen actively apply the practice of involving stakeholders in management with opportunities for government participation in the process of social entrepreneurship development. On the other hand, the United States can be an example for Europe to expand the scope of social enterprises and the types of legal forms of such enterprises, as well as the use of government contracts to purchase products." The different sources of financing for social enterprises (SEs) and the tools specific to each are shown in table 2.4 below.

Source of Financing SEs	**Tools of Financing Employed**
Social Entrepreneur	Equity capital (owner's equity)
General population	Crowdfunding
Private investors	Venture capital, Angel investments, Impact investments
Charitable and public organizations	Fellowships, Grand challenges
Large businesses	Corporate social responsibility (CSR) grants
International organizations	Grants, Social impact bonds
Banks	Loans
Credit unions/Microfinance institutions	Microcredit

Table 2.4: The Main Sources and Instruments of Financing Social Enterprises
Source: Akbulaev, Et Al, 2019

In the above table, crowdfunding is an open call on the internet to raise financial resources in the form of cash donations, sometimes in exchange for future products, services, or rewards (Akbulaev et al., 2019). Also, there are some "innovative instruments," such as social impact bonds and impact investing. Khanna defines social impact bonds as a "new approach to social programs, aimed at raising funds from charitable organizations and the investors for financing of preventive social programs, while impact investing is focused on making business profit with measurable social results, while solving the social problems of poor and marginalized populations" (Khanna, 2018).

Akbulaev et al maintain that the "existence of such social enterprises without additional state and public support is impossible". They call for enhanced cooperation between key partners, involving the government authorities and local governments for regulatory support, large businesses for Corporate Social Responsibility (CSR) support and mentoring, media for promotion of social activities of the social businesses, the educational institutions for training the social entrepreneurs, and public organizations working directly with the public with the purpose of clarifying the value of key principles of social enterprises.

The blending of government, philanthropic, and private funds for social businesses has led to the "blended finance" approach, which has gained traction lately. Blended finance was first mentioned as an option for financing development globally in the Addis Ababa Action Agenda of the Third International Conference of Financing for Development (UN, 2015). It defined blended finance as a mechanism "which combines concessional public finance with non-concessional private finance and expertise from the public and private sector, special-purpose vehicles, non-recourse project financing, risk mitigation instruments and pooled funding structures". In the context of Sustainable Development Goals (SDGs), the Organization for Economic Cooperation and Development (OECD) defined blended finance as "the strategic use of development finance for the mobilization of additional finance towards the SDGs in developing countries" (OECD, 2018). The consultation paper of the Blended Finance Task Force quoted the United Nations' estimate of around $6 trillion per year required to achieve the Sustainable Development Goals by 2030, with a $2-3 trillion annual gap (Taskforce, B.F., 2018). The consultation paper further mentioned that "development capital in the form of aid and public funds can, at most, cover half of this gap and asserted that by de-risking some of these investments, blended finance can allow the private sector to participate, potentially capturing over $1 trillion in additional annual investment potential."

The use of blended concessional financing has acquired significance in the post-COVID pandemic economy, with the International Finance Corporation (IFC) and other development finance institutions ramping up their efforts to deploy blended concessional finance solutions in response to the pandemic. Sierra-Escalante and Karlin have found that in the post-pandemic economy, "the private companies have been significantly impacted by changes to market conditions, including deteriorating global demand, flight of finance (including foreign direct investment and portfolio equity), supply chain disruptions, reduced trade, and declines in commodity prices". But they have also found pockets of opportunity. They note that "some private firms in the health supply and services sector are playing an expanded role in fighting the pandemic" (Sierra-Escalante & Karlin, 2021).

Several Development Finance Institutions (DFIs), including IFC, have instituted emergency support programs for the private sector. As per Sierra-Escalante and Karlin, these have "focused initially on near-term liquidity issues such as trade finance and working capital, supporting Small and Medium Enterprises (SMEs) and corporate clients, and in many cases working through local financial intermediaries." Financial intermediaries, when provided with adequate support or risk mitigation, can help in filling the finance gap that resulted from COVID-19 by ensuring that lines of credit are made available. In higher-risk situations, such as in uncertain market conditions during the COVID-19 pandemic and in underdeveloped financial markets in least developed countries, the level of investment risks can exceed the risk-bearing capacity of both private-sector investors and DFIs. Sierra-Escalante and Karlin further argue that "blended concessional finance can be very important to bring the risk-return profile to a range that can attract other investors, facilitate additional projects with important development impacts, and allow a significant portion of the pandemic response to be directed to lower-income and fragile countries. Blended concessional finance can also help ensure that, as firms are stabilized and renewed but remain exposed to significant financial and operational risks, projects can still address critical issues of inclusion, gender equality, and climate sustainability" (Sierra-Escalante & Karlin, 2021).

Kiiza, et al, argue that "while the global political economy has gravitated towards an ideology of inclusion, it can hardly gain traction without increased development financing, and blended finance seems to make sense in this case" (Kiiza, et al, 2019). They have examined the differential expectations of various investors in blended financing. According to them, concessional lenders use their resources to maximize global power and influence. "Philanthropic donors invoke the logic of corporate social responsibility to maximize their developmental relevance. Aid recipients, such as Uganda and Tanzania, seek to maximize country-specific developmental outcomes (such as maternal and newborn health). The unifying denominator, the new politics of aid, is defined as the struggle by different actors to shape today's development policy space in furtherance of their cherished values, interests or preferences, whether they are commercial or ideological."

As far as social enterprises are concerned, a lack of appropriate funding is a major bottleneck faced by them. As per Bugg-Levine, et al, "some of the more forward-thinking foundations and social investors have realized that the current methods of financing social enterprises are inefficient, for the enterprises and themselves, and have started working to broaden the access to capital" (Bugg-Levine, et al, 2012).

According to the USAID blended finance roadmap, blended finance mobilized $27 billion in private capital by 2015, with annual growth of 22% (USAID, 2019). In a study of social enterprises and investors in Indonesia, it was found that although blended finance bridged a crucial funding gap, many social enterprises were not investment-ready, lacked sector focus, and had limited connections to social finance (Soukhasing et al, 2017).

Basile and Dutra, in their survey of blended finance facilities globally, examined blended finance transactions across sectors, as shown in figure 2.7 below.

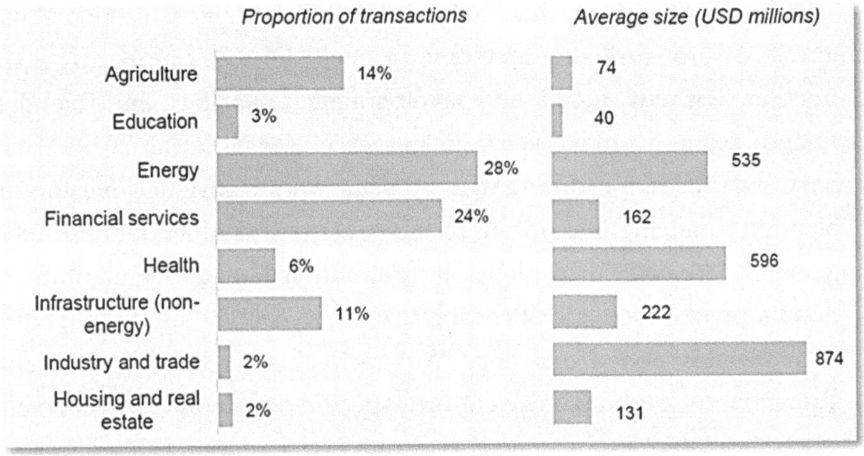

Figure 2.7: Number And Size of Blended Finance Transactions by Sector
Source: Basile and Dutra, 2019

Basile and Dutra found that 44% of blended finance transactions targeted business enterprises, mostly small and medium businesses covering the social enterprises, but had focused largely on energy and financial services sectors, with only 6% transactions dealing with health (Basile & Dutra, 2019), as shown in the above figure (figure 6). The healthcare social enterprises also face additional problems in fund raising as "public health professionals still need to fully embrace businesses (for profit or not) as partners in promoting health and well-being, in achievement of SDG-3", and, on the other hand "businesses (especially SEs) do not yet see public health institutions and practitioners as potential partners in their work with communities" (Macassa, 2021).

Clearly, there are too few healthcare blended finance initiatives financing healthcare social entrepreneurs, and hence most of the literature on blended finance misses the unique needs of healthcare social entrepreneurs addressing the third Sustainable Development Goal.

In a recently published white paper by the Government of India's think tank, NITI *Aayog*, blended finance was identified as a key driver of new capital into high-impact healthcare solutions and projects (NITI *Aayog*, 2022). The white paper also listed a few recent healthcare blended finance initiatives launched to support healthcare social enterprises in India. These new initiatives need to be studied further to generate evidence on whether these financing structures comprehensively address the business and financial risks faced by social enterprises in India.

2.5. Summary

If businesses focus only on the economic bottom line, it will not be sustainable in the long run because of potential negative impacts on the physical and social environments in which businesses operate (Wall & Gong, 2001; Krajnc & Glavic, 2005). Sustainable development of business as a core business value has acquired greater significance with the UN adopting the Sustainable Development Goals (Williams, 2015; Scheyvens et al., 2016) and urging the business leaders globally to join the initiative through Economic-Social-Governance (ESG) lensed investing (Lokuwaduge, 2016).

The idea of sustainable development for businesses evolved into a framework of the triple bottom line (Elkington, 1997; Svensson et al., 2016 and 2018). The triple bottom line (TBL) framework was further adopted as an investment tool through the "Environment-Social-Governance" (ESG) investing mechanism (The Global Compact, 2004; Armstrong, 2020; Foubert, 2020).

However, the ESG framework is more applicable to mainstream commercial investments (Bertolotti, 2020), which may not be suitable for social enterprises (SEs). This is because the SEs are not purely commercial entities and face other challenges, such as high failure rates of social business models and the issue of mission drift (Massarsky, 2006; Foster & Bradach, 2005).

SEs are key to sustainable development as they overlap with the economic and social environments (Rahdari et al., 2016; Terziev & Arabska, 2017; Macassa, 2021). This overlap leads to the flow of both commercial and non-commercial (philanthropic and public) funds into SEs. Thus, blended financing, which combines commercial and non-commercial funds into a single investment, becomes critical for financing SEs (Kiiza et al., 2019; Sierra-Escalante & Karlin, 2021).

In summary, while industries focus primarily on economic impact, with social and environmental impact as an additionality of their economic activity, non-profits focus primarily on social and/or environmental impact, with economic impact as an additionality. It is only the social enterprises that focus on all three aspects of the triple bottom line as their primary focus. Also, social enterprises get blended funding, which is a mix of commercial investment and philanthropic/public funding, whereas industries get commercial investments, which is showing an ESG lens of investing lately. On the other hand, non-profits receive only philanthropic and public funding, with no commercial investments, as their activities are essentially non-commercial.

The literature review also shows that a research gap exists for a comprehensive blended financing framework to evaluate commercial, philanthropic, and public investments in SEs. The ESG framework, which guides commercial investments into sustainable businesses, does not mention the de-risking role of pubic and philanthropic funds in a blended financing scenario. On the other hand, the blended finance literature discusses the de-risking role of public and philanthropic funds in attracting commercial investments, but it misses how these non-commercial investment decisions are made or how funders reconcile economic, environmental, and social priorities and expenditures. The literature is also silent on any common or mutually supporting investment decision-making tool guiding commercial, philanthropic, and public funding of SEs. There is also a very specific research gap on healthcare SEs, which has become important in the post-COVID pandemic world (Basile & Dutra, 2019). Hence, the literature review shows a lack of sufficient research to determine whether the role of philanthropic and public funds in healthcare SEs is limited to de-risking commercial investments or whether they also play other roles.

Chapter 3 | Methodology

3.1. Overview of the Research Problem

Increasingly, it is evident that the investments required for sustainable development – balancing economic, social, and environmental progress – are substantial and cannot be met by public or private entities on their own. The challenge is to find ways and means to bring together private investments and public funds working in the social sector. This is where the social enterprises play an important role, operating at the junction of the commercial and social sectors. This study focuses on this hybrid approach of combining public and private resources for social good – broadly termed blended financing.

Given the shortage of research on healthcare social enterprises and their use of blended finance, this research aims to study the risks perceived by social enterprises and investors and whether blended finance can address those risks in the Indian healthcare context. The study also explores whether social entrepreneurs need more than just financing to address their risk and access-to-capital issues, and to scale the health and social impact of their enterprises.

3.2. Operationalization of Theoretical Constructs

As the literature review shows, the use of blended finance by social enterprises for sustainable development is a recent phenomenon, and its use in healthcare is further limited. At this stage, it is important to understand the existing practices and related issues in the context of recent trends and challenges. The case study method helps in developing the conceptual model of healthcare social enterprises in relation to their financing and social impact.

As per the framework presented in figure 2.1 in the literature review section previously, industries focus primarily on economic impact, with social and environmental impacts being an additionality to their economic activity. On the other hand, the non-profits focus primarily on social and/or environmental impact, with economic impact being an additionality. It is only the social enterprises that focus on all three aspects of the triple bottom line as their primary focus. Also, social enterprises get blended funding, which is a mix of commercial investment and philanthropic/public funding, whereas industries get commercial investments, which is showing an ESG lens of investing lately. On the other hand, non-profits receive only philanthropic and public funding, with no commercial investments, as their activities are essentially non-commercial.

The evolving theoretical framework for the research thus examines the healthcare enterprises in terms of the business and financial risks they face, how they address social impact and sustainability, and the role blended finance plays in this. These elements in the framework and their interrelationships are depicted in figure 3.1 below.

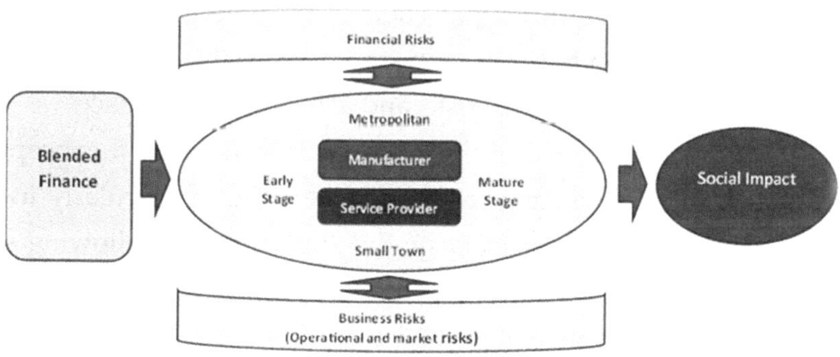

Figure 3.1: Analytical Framework for Blended Finance, Risks, Social Enterprises, and Impact

The elements discussed above are then seen in the context of the stage the businesses are at (early stage versus mature stage), the locational context (big metro city versus small town), and the type of product/service (equipment manufacturers versus service providers). The analytical framework depicted in the figure above serves as the basis for the Framework Analysis used to develop the conceptual framework for blended finance, risks, healthcare social enterprises, and social impact.

3.3. Research Purpose and Questions

Given the shortage of research on healthcare social enterprises and their use of blended finance for growth, this research aims to study the risks faced by healthcare social enterprises and how blended finance can address those risks in the Indian healthcare context. Given that blended finance, especially in the healthcare sector, is at a nascent stage in India and globally, the study develops a conceptual framework of risk, returns, and impact for healthcare social enterprises, employing a grounded theory approach. Because of grounded theory, the research does not start with any explicit hypothesis but has the following broad research questions.

- How do social enterprises address social impact and business viability?
- What are the risks of healthcare social enterprises in India?
- How does the mixing of commercial investments and donor grants in blended financing structures enable healthcare social enterprises to address risks and achieve social impact?

The primary objective of the research is to develop a conceptual model of blended financing for social enterprises, particularly in the health sector in India. Particularly, the study has the following sub-objectives:

- Explore the financing challenges faced by healthcare social enterprises in India and the financial and advisory support they need to sustain and expand their operations while achieving social and health impact.

- Study the implications of mixing different types of capital through blended financing on the business and financial risk of the healthcare social enterprises in India and on the social and health impact achieved by such enterprises.

3.4. Research Design

The research follows a diagnostic research design, investigating the underlying phenomenon of how blended finance enables social enterprises to address risks and social impact. A qualitative case-study approach is adopted to come up with a conceptual model. This method is chosen because qualitative case study helps in "exploration of a phenomenon within some particular context through various data sources, and it undertakes the exploration through variety of lenses in order to reveal multiple facets of the phenomenon" (Baxter & Jack, 2008). Also, in case study, "a real-time phenomenon is explored within its naturally occurring context, with the consideration that context will create a difference" (Kaarbo and Beasley, 1999). As per Halinen and Tornroos, a case strategy involves "an intensive study of one or small number of business networks, where multiple sources of evidence are used to develop a holistic description of the network and where the network refers to a set of companies (and potentially other organizations) connected to each other for the purpose of doing business" (Halinen and Tornroos, 2005). Jarvensivu and Tornroos also suggest that case studies are suitable for "exploring business-to-business relationships and networks" (Jarvensivu and Tornroos, 2010).

3.5. Population, Sample and Participant Selection

Four case studies were developed covering different healthcare social enterprises that have adopted blended finance to de-risk their operations and accelerate healthcare social impact in India. The social enterprises were selected for the case studies from a limited universe of 21 such healthcare social enterprises in India that have adopted blended finance for more than one financial year, to mitigate their business and financial risks and to accelerate their enterprise, as well as the health impact achieved by them, USAID-funded *SAMRIDH* blended finance initiative (Chakraborty & Rao, 2022). The types of healthcare social enterprises included in the sample are shown in table 3.1 below.

	Early Stage	**Matured Stage**
Manufacturer	Case Study 1 (High-end Diagnostic Equipment enterprise)	Case Study 2 (Portable Diagnostic Equipment enterprise)
Service Provider	Case Study 3 (Primary healthcare enterprise)	Case Study 4 (Healthcare enterprise)

Table 3.1: Type of Healthcare Social Enterprises Included in the Sample

Given the two types of healthcare social enterprises (manufacturers and healthcare service providers) and the early or the mature stage of business, one enterprise was chosen from each type, based on the criteria of "substantial blended finance experience" and consent to share information regarding their journey.

The sample did not include healthcare social enterprises that have not experienced blended finance in their financing mix or have adopted blended finance for less than 1 year.

3.6. Instrumentation and Data Collection Procedures

Data collection involved In-Depth interviews (IDIs) of the healthcare social entrepreneurs, using an open-ended checklist. In addition, project documents and financial statements of such enterprises were also studied to develop the case studies. The data collection plan for each of the proposed case studies developed for this research, is described in table 3.2 below.

	Data Source	Key Information Collected from the Source	Tool for Data Collection
1.	Healthcare Social Entrepreneur	Mission of the enterprise, history, current operations and future plans, risks and challenges faced, mitigation strategies adopted, how the risks and social impact are addressed, experience with blended finance.	In-depth interview (IDI), using structured but open-ended checklist
2.	Documents related to the enterprise, including website contents	Mission of the enterprise, history, current operations and future plans, social and health impacts, experience with blended finance.	Document review

Table 3.2: Data Collection Plan for Each Case Study
Source: Author

The human subjects in this research were the entrepreneurs who owned the social enterprises studied. Ethical considerations are explained below:

- **Informed consent:** Informed consent was obtained at the beginning of the interview, in which the academic nature of the research was clearly explained to the respondent using a structured consent form. Permission was also taken to record the conversation with assurance of masking personal and company identifiers.
- **Confidentiality:** The respondent was assured of confidentiality, explaining that the respondent's name and personal identifiers, company name, product brand name and location of the enterprise would be masked.
- **Privacy and being:** The in-depth interview was conducted in private, in the entrepreneur's office, without any third person's presence, to enable the respondent to speak freely.
- **Being sensitive and respectful:** The researcher was sensitive and respectful toward the respondent, appreciating the entrepreneur's vision and efforts and expressing gratitude for sharing it with the researcher.

3.7. Data Analysis

As the primary objective of this research is to come up with a conceptual model of blended financing of social enterprises, data analysis was primarily based on Grounded Theory Analysis. It was supplemented with a Narrative Analysis of the in-depth interviews (IDIs). The data obtained from the IDIs and document analysis were further categorized for the four case studies, using Framework Analysis for interpreting the commonalities and differences against the different contexts of the case studies. All this was synthesized to develop the conceptual model of blended financing for social enterprises in the healthcare context. The data collection and analysis process is depicted in figure 3.3 below.

3.8. Research Design Limitations

As stated earlier, the phenomenon of blended finance, especially in the context of financing startup and growth-stage healthcare social enterprises, is nascent in India and globally. Hence, this research was constrained by unavoidable factors.

The major limitation of this research is the limited universe of healthcare social enterprises adopting blended finance approaches to finance their operations. Although this is sufficient to build a suggestive conceptual model of financing for social enterprises that addresses sustainability and impact, it is insufficient to conclusively test and establish the model.

Also, almost all healthcare social enterprises adopting blended finance approaches are established as private limited companies or limited liability partnerships. Hence, their financial statements are confidential and not publicly available. The researcher had to rely on what the enterprise owners shared, and the information could not be impudently validated. So, the research can suggest a conceptual framework for the financing and sustainability of social enterprises, especially in the healthcare sector, but cannot conclusively prove the model or whether the adoption of blended finance improves financial sustainability and social impact in the medium to long run.

The healthcare social enterprises adopted blended finance approaches after the COVID pandemic and have less than three years of experience with such arrangements. This time frame is insufficient to test and establish sustainability, but it is sufficient to observe the trend and determine whether they are on the path to sustainability.

Finally, the healthcare sector is unique, with strong supplier-induced demand driven by information asymmetry between suppliers and consumers. Also, a large portion of healthcare consists of social and merit goods, for which market forces do not work well. A sector characterized by such market failures is very unlike other industrial segments, and hence the framework suggested for healthcare social enterprises may not be readily applicable to other sectors. However, as the research concerns the financing of sustainable goals, the conceptual framework will be applicable to other social goods, such as education, food and nutrition, the welfare of special population segments, and environmental conservation.

3.9. Conclusion

This research adopts a qualitative approach to develop a conceptual model of how blended finance addresses the business and financial risks faced by healthcare social enterprises in their quest for economic sustainability and social impact. The method relies on framework analysis and grounded theory, using content and narrative analysis of the in-depth interviews and document reviews. Finally, a conceptual framework is suggested linking blended finance and social enterprises to sustainable development outcomes, which would need to be further tested in future regarding its relevance in the context of healthcare social enterprises.

Chapter 4 | Results

4.1. SAMRIDH Healthcare Blended Finance Initiative in India

Among very few blended finance facilities working globally, especially in healthcare, *the SAMRIDH* blended finance initiative in India is a unique arrangement set up by USAID, the Government of India, and other partners during the COVID pandemic. It was originally designed to financially support the adoption of healthcare innovations in the more than 20,000 hospitals that formed part of the ambitious health insurance program in India, providing cashless healthcare to the 500 million bottom-of-the-pyramid population. Its uniqueness lies not in creating a blended finance "fund", but in establishing a blended finance "partnership" that brings together providers of concessional capital and investment capital, along with market enablers such as apex engineering colleges, government bodies, incubators, and accelerators.

As per a case study published by Chakraborty and Rao (2022), the *SAMRIDH* blended finance facility comprises two notional pools: (a) the investment pool, and (b) the grants pool. As per the case study on *SAMRIDH* (Chakraborty & Rao, 2022), "these are notional pools as funds remain with the individual funding entity, which directly invests/grants the funds to the social enterprises as decided in the advisory committee." The case study further states that "these notional pools are coordinated by the Technical Support Unit (TSU) funded by *SAMRIDH*, which also acts as the secretariat for the advisory committee. The TSU builds the investment pipeline, evaluates the business case from each proposal submitted by the applying social enterprises, and monitors the progress towards the development outcomes." A grant of $30 million is held by the TSU itself, disbursed as per the recommendations of the advisory committee of *SAMRIDH.* There is a separate grant pool held by the Indian Institute of Technology, Delhi (IITD), which is an apex institute run by the Indian government and part of the *SAMRIDH* partnership. The commercial capital providers include commercial banks (IndusInd and Axis), impact investment firms such as Caspian, and development finance institutions such as the US Government's Development Finance Corporation (DFC). Together, the *SAMRIDH* facility boasts a commitment of more than $300 million in grants and loans. As per the case study, "all the funding partners are members of the advisory committee. In addition, there are also Government of India representatives on the committee to ensure *SAMRIDH-supported* entities adhere to the national pandemic response strategies and policies." This is depicted in figure 4.1 below.

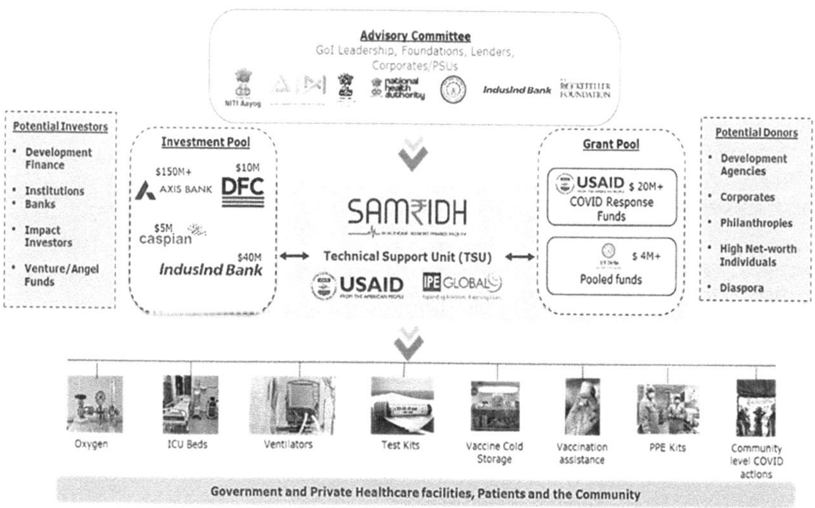

Figure 4.1: SAMRIDH Blended Finance Facility in India
Source: Chakraborty and Rao, 2022

The case study also mentions that "the social enterprises supported under *SAMRIDH* include entities engaged in providing products, services and solutions related to oxygen, critical care beds, ventilators, COVID test kits, vaccine cold storage facilities and equipment, vaccination assistance, protective kits for health personnel and patients and community level actions involving awareness building and education." By mid-2022, there were 21 *SAMRIDH-supported* healthcare social enterprises, which increased to more than 30 by early 2024.

Brandeis University also developed a case study on *SAMRIDH,* which clearly states that "blended finance initiatives like *SAMRIDH* can be a positive tool for creating investment opportunities and promoting tri-sector collaboration between public, private, and philanthropic organizations towards scaling impact for development" (Carlson et al., 2024).

For this research, four case studies were developed covering different healthcare social enterprises that have adopted blended finance to de-risk their operations and accelerate healthcare social impact in India. The social enterprises were selected for the case studies from the limited universe of around 30 *SAMRIDH-supported* enterprises in India that have adopted blended finance to mitigate their business and financial risks and to accelerate their business and the health impact achieved by their enterprises. The researcher has used publicly available information, open-source publications and primary data collected by the researcher. These four case studies are presented in the following sections.

4.2. Case Study 1: High-End Diagnostic Equipment Manufacturing Enterprise

The first healthcare social enterprise studied was a high-end diagnostic equipment business, an early-stage enterprise manufacturing high-end medical equipment, in a large metropolitan city in southern India. It is a professional-owned enterprise, with the lead promoter an engineer with decades of experience in the high-end medical diagnostics industry and extensive industry and professional connections.

The enterprise was established in 2017 as a private limited company, meaning it is not publicly listed and, as a result, its financial statements are not publicly available. So, the researcher had to rely on information and documents shared by the entrepreneur during the interaction, with the assurance that the personal and company identities would be masked for the purpose of the research.

The business and financial model, sustainability and impact achieved, risks faced, and the role blended finance played in the enterprise are described in the following sections.

4.2.1. Business Model

Their business model aims to improve healthcare access while maintaining commercial viability. As per the enterprise website, "the enterprise's vision is to make MRI affordable and accessible using its technology called next-gen MRI for vulnerable populations."

The enterprise has developed a next-generation MRI scanner that is more affordable and accessible. It is a make-in-India, dry, 1.5 Tesla MRI magnet, with dimensions especially suitable for the average Indian physique and body size. The MRI scanner has unique features that set it apart from competitors. As per the entrepreneur, the machine "does not use any expensive liquid cryogens" and is "extremely tolerant of electrical and environmental disruptions." The enterprise has filed patents for its technology. The equipment is approved by the Central Drugs Control Organization of India (CDSCO). The enterprise has filed a patent for software to improve MRI film quality.

The enterprise focuses on making MRI technology accessible in small and medium-sized towns and cities, and in remote areas. To make it affordable in these areas, the enterprise aims to reduce the cost of MRI scanners through innovative design and local manufacturing. As per the entrepreneur, "Initially, we are planning at somewhere around ₹ 3.5 crores per machine ($ 400,000), and once we scale up or once we start scaling, we are planning at ₹ 3 crores ($ 350,000)." This is comparable to the price of similar equipment in the local market.

The enterprise is looking at staggered market penetration. It plans to install a few scanners initially in some selected hospitals to gather feedback before wider deployment. As per the entrepreneur, "You need all this. You would like to put some 3 or 4 scanners in a few sites and then get some feedback from them."

The enterprise is working with organizations such as reputed Indian corporate philanthropies that run their own hospitals. These charity hospitals serve as testing sites for the few MRI machines the enterprise has developed.

This business model combines technological innovation, cost-effective manufacturing, and a focus on underserved markets to deliver a commercially viable solution to improve access to MRI technology. By addressing both affordability and accessibility of MRI scanners, the enterprise aims to expand the market for these essential diagnostic tools while improving healthcare outcomes in underserved areas.

4.2.2. Financial Model

The enterprise uses a mix of funding sources, including concessional capital, venture capital and commercial investments. The major source of concessional capital is from *the SAMRIDH* blended finance initiative, in the form of a Recoverable Grant. As per information shared by the entrepreneur, the enterprise has received a Recoverable Grant of ₹ 1.2 crores ($150,000). As per the documents shared by the enterprise, they used this recoverable grant to mobilize additional investments worth 13.5-times the monetary value. This indicates a hybrid form of financing that combines elements of grants and loans.

The enterprise considers economies of scale and the resulting cost reductions once full-scale sales operations begin. The enterprise emphasizes cost reduction across both production and operations. Key words used by the entrepreneur during the discussion were "cheaper, affordable". Their pitch to the customer is that the machine "consumes less power" and "does not use any expensive liquid cryogens," thereby resulting in lower life-cycle cost. There is a strong localization focus involving "Make in India", offering lower-cost options than foreign products.

This financial model combines elements of social impact investing (using recoverable grants) with a traditional technology startup approach of developing an innovative product for a large, underserved market. The focus on cost reduction across manufacturing and operations is central to their strategy to make MRI technology more accessible and affordable.

The model appears designed to achieve financial sustainability while addressing a significant social need. By leveraging initial grant funding to attract further investment and focusing on cost-effective production and operation, the enterprise aims to create a commercially viable product that can also achieve significant social impact in healthcare accessibility.

4.2.3. Social Impact and Sustainable Development

The enterprise aims to make MRI technology more accessible, especially in underserved areas, by deploying it in remote locations, including smaller towns. The enterprise is developing a more affordable MRI scanner to reduce the cost barrier. As per the entrepreneur quoted earlier, "initially we are planning at somewhere around ₹ 3.5 crores per machine ($ 400,000), and once we scale up or once we start scaling, we are planning at ₹ 3 crores ($ 350,000)." Their MRI scanner is designed to have lower operating costs (about 50% lower) over its life cycle by consuming less power and avoiding expensive liquid cryogens.

The technology developed by the enterprise aims to address the limited availability of advanced diagnostic equipment in India.

Example: As per the entrepreneur, "less than 20% of hospitals in India have advanced equipment for detecting arrhythmia or coronary heart disease." By making MRI technology more accessible, they are contributing to the expansion of healthcare infrastructure in underserved areas. The entrepreneur very clearly mentioned that "to address accessibility issues, there is a need for more affordable alternatives, especially considering the government's 'Make in India' initiative." Their technology also helps in addressing the rising tide of chronic illnesses in India. The entrepreneur has this in mind and said, "India, with its large population, faces a rising tide of chronic illnesses. The demand for advanced imaging tools like MRI is growing, yet access remains limited due to high costs and infrastructure challenges."

Keeping in mind the sustainability aspect, the MRI scanner is designed to be more environmentally friendly and sustainable. The equipment is light, compact and relatively mobile, and tolerant of electrical and environmental disruptions. As mentioned by the entrepreneur, "the company is also a white-category company with zero discharge of pollutants."

The enterprise is dedicated to the localization theme. The enterprise takes pride in developing and manufacturing the MRI scanners locally in India, contributing to local economic development. Also, by developing the technology locally, they are reducing dependency on imported medical equipment.

Their work aligns with government initiatives to improve healthcare access and promote local manufacturing, especially considering the government's "Make in India" initiative.

The enterprise's approach to social impact and sustainable development is centered on addressing a critical healthcare need (access to MRI technology) through technological innovation and a business model that prioritizes affordability and accessibility. By developing a more cost-effective, environmentally friendly, and locally manufactured MRI scanner, they aim to improve diagnostic capabilities in underserved areas, potentially leading to better health outcomes and reduced healthcare costs in the long term.

Their work contributes to several Sustainable Development Goals (SDGs), particularly SDG 3 (Good Health and Well-being) and SDG 9 (Industry, Innovation, and Infrastructure). By making advanced medical technology more accessible, they are working to reduce health inequalities and improve overall healthcare quality in India and, potentially, beyond.

4.2.4. Business and Financial Risks

The business and financial risks faced by the enterprise are discussed below, taking into account its manufacturing status, location in a metropolitan city, and early-stage status.

4.2.4.1. Business Risks

The enterprise faces regulatory risk as it needs to maintain compliance with regulatory standards. The device is currently approved by the Central Drugs Standard Control Organization (CDSCO) under the Ministry of Health, Government of India. Related to this is the technology risk as the enterprise is developing a novel MRI technology. This carries inherent risks of technical challenges or unforeseen issues. Related to this is the intellectual property (IP) risk. While the enterprise has filed patents, there is always a risk of IP infringement.

Being a new technology, there is a risk of market acceptance. There is also a risk that hospitals and healthcare providers may be hesitant to adopt a new, unproven technology. To test the waters, the enterprise is currently not having any sales but putting three or four machines in a few sites on a "pay-as-you-use" basis and trying to get some feedback from the users.

There is a potential competitive risk, with a high likelihood that established MRI manufacturers will respond with their own low-cost solutions. This also creates challenges for future scaling, especially as established market players may resist rapid expansion.

4.2.4.2. Financial Risks

There is a funding risk due to reliance on grants and recoverable grants. This is because grants are one-time funding, and there is no certainty of continued grant funding in the future. Added to this is the issue of a high leverage ratio of 13.5, which is riding on cash infusions from grants. This further increases the financing risk. The high leverage ratio indicates significant expectations for additional cash, which may or may not materialize.

While the entrepreneur mentions "cheaper/affordable" as a key product feature, the planned price reduction strategy may impact profitability. Also, keeping production costs low enough to offer an affordable product while maintaining quality can be challenging. In addition, while the product is designed to have lower operating costs, unforeseen issues can erode this advantage, increasing the risk of operating costs.

The significant Research and Development investment may take time to recover, especially with a lower-priced product. This is indicated by the long development process from 2016 to the present, as shared by the entrepreneur, and sales have still not started. The phased market-entry approach may also delay revenue generation.

These risks highlight the complex challenges the enterprise faces in bringing an innovative medical device to market while maintaining affordability and quality. The enterprise's success will depend on effectively managing these risks through careful planning, robust quality control, strategic partnerships, and flexible financial management.

4.2.5. How Blended Finance Is Helping the Healthcare Social Enterprise

Blended finance is enabling the enterprise to address various aspects of its business model, including risks, financial sustainability, social impact, and sustainable development, as explained below.

- **Addressing Risks:** Blended finance helps mitigate financial risks through cash infusions from *SAMRIDH*, totalling ₹1,20,00,000 ($150,000) in recoverable grants. This initial funding helps mitigate early-stage financial risks by providing capital without immediate repayment pressure. The support from *SAMRIDH* and potentially other partners helps validate market potential, reducing market acceptance risk by financing additional machines that clients may not purchase, and allowing the enterprise to adjust specifications to market needs. The Grants also help in the phased development of the enterprise by financing the initial stages when there is no revenue.
- **Financial Sustainability:** Blended finance, especially the grant component, helped the enterprise leverage 13.5 times commercial investments. The grant covers critical operational costs, supporting financial sustainability in the early stages.
- **Scalability:** The initial support enables the enterprise to develop and refine its product, potentially leading to a more scalable business model.
- **Social Impact:** The enterprise's vision is to make MRI affordable and accessible for vulnerable populations through its next-gen MRI technology. Blended finance supports the development of technology that can improve healthcare access in underserved areas. With less than 20% of hospitals in India equipped with advanced equipment for detecting arrhythmias or coronary heart disease, the grants help the enterprise address this significant healthcare gap. The blended finance approach also allows the enterprise to focus on developing an affordable product without immediate profit pressure.

- **Sustainable Development:** The support enables the enterprise to develop sustainable technology that is "extremely tolerant of electrical and environmental disruptions" and "does not use any expensive liquid cryogens." As the entrepreneur mentioned, the enterprise has emerged as a "white-category company" with zero discharge of pollutants, indicating a focus on environmental sustainability. While not explicitly mentioned, the project aligns with SDG-3 (Good Health and Well-being) and SDG-9 (Industry, Innovation, and Infrastructure).
- **Enabling Innovation:** The blended finance approach provides the necessary capital for innovative research and development that might be too risky for traditional financing. The funding also supports the development of proprietary technology.
- **Market Expansion:** Blended finance has supported market expansion, and the enterprise team is in advanced discussions and has commenced distribution of the MRI machine in the north-eastern Indian state of Assam. Blended finance supports expansion into underserved markets by subsidizing initial market acquisition, penetration, and logistics costs, while facilitating partnerships, such as the one mentioned with corporate philanthropy.

It seems that blended finance is crucial for the enterprise's development of innovative, affordable MRI technology. It provides the necessary capital to support research and development and initial operations while allowing the enterprise to focus on its social impact goals. This approach enables the enterprise to address significant healthcare challenges in India and potentially globally, balancing the need for financial sustainability with social impact and sustainable development. The blended finance model helps de-risk the early stages of the project, making it more attractive for future commercial investments and supporting the long-term viability of the enterprise's mission to improve healthcare accessibility.

4.2.6. Conclusion

The business and finance model of the high-end diagnostic equipment manufacturing that the enterprise studied enables it to navigate the complex challenges of developing and deploying advanced medical technology in a developing market context. It balances the need for technological innovation and affordability with financial viability and scalability.

The model demonstrates how blended financing can support high-risk, high-impact ventures in the healthcare sector, potentially leading to transformative changes in healthcare accessibility and quality in developing regions. By de-risking the early stages of development and deployment, blended finance creates a pathway for future commercial investment and long-term sustainability while ensuring that social impact goals remain central to the venture.

4.3. Case Study 2: Portable Low-Cost Diagnostic Equipment Manufacturing Enterprise

The second healthcare social enterprise studied was a portable, low-cost diagnostic equipment enterprise, a mature-stage enterprise manufacturing innovative medical devices, in a small north Indian town. The enterprise was founded in 2016 by a group of fresh engineering graduates with a passion for bringing affordable healthcare to people in far-flung areas of the Himalayan region they were in, primarily focused on emergency medical care. They started as a start-up but soon acquired a respected clientele, including the Indian Army and the Indian Space Research Organization, where their portable pocket-ECG plays a significant life-saving role in the harsh Himalayan terrain and the space environment (for the planned Indian manned space mission).

The business and financial model, sustainability and impact achieved, risks faced, and the role of blended finance in the business are described in the following sections.

4.3.1. Business Model

The enterprise is more like a research and development laboratory, focused on creating cutting-edge healthcare technologies. Their flagship product is a low-cost, portable, battery-free ECG device. As per the lead entrepreneur, "the enterprise has developed a branded ECG device, a pocket-sized innovation that swiftly diagnoses life-threatening cardiac events." There are several variations of the device, including Military Grade, Neo, Pro, Legacy, and Alfa Test.

The enterprise sells the Device ECG device directly to consumers and through partnerships with distributors and healthcare providers. While the device is priced at ₹7,200 ($85) on Amazon, the enterprise also has partnerships with companies in Kenya, Tanzania, and Somalia for distribution in Africa. Furthermore, they have deployed devices through private clinics, government healthcare facilities, and phlebotomists in India.

Besides selling these devices, the enterprise also offers additional healthcare services, including ECG reporting services, corporate screening programs, and heart attack management systems.

The enterprise actively collaborates with various stakeholders to expand its reach and impact. The collaboration with the *SAMRIDH* blended finance initiative brought them financial assistance, business advisory, and market access support. This partnership led to significant device deployment and market expansion. The infusion of funds from *SAMRIDH* provided the enterprise with new capital for rapid expansion in India and globally. The enterprise also partners with governments and NGOs.

The enterprise aims to expand its reach globally, focusing on making the pocket-ECG device accessible in underserved communities worldwide. As reported by the entrepreneur, "the enterprise has established its presence in 12 countries in the African subcontinent." In India, the enterprise plans to deploy the device in public health facilities nationwide, including in smaller towns, semi-urban, rural areas, and villages.

The enterprise is on a rapid revenue growth trajectory. While the revenues before the *SAMRIDH* funds infusion in 2021 were ₹ 23,686,095 ($ 285,000), it registered a 120% growth post *SAMRIDH* funds infusion, reaching ₹ 52,019,000 ($ 627,000). This resulted in a transition to profitability from a negative EBIDTA of - ₹ 1,100,000 (-$13,253) to a positive EBIDTA of ₹ 2,800,000 ($33,700).

The enterprise's mission is to provide accessible and affordable healthcare solutions. As reported by the entrepreneur, their devices are operating in more than 14 countries and have enabled "diagnosing one million heartbeats and saving more than 200,000 lives."

In summary, the business model combines product development and sales with service provision, strategic partnerships, and a focus on global expansion. Their blended financing strategy and commitment to social impact are key elements of their approach to making life-saving cardiac care more accessible and affordable worldwide. The enterprise leverages both commercial and philanthropic funding to achieve its ambitious goals.

4.3.2. Financial Model

The enterprise utilizes a mix of funding sources. The enterprise obtained concessional capital in the form of seed grants from *SAMRIDH* and Let'sVenture. The enterprise then leveraged these seed grants to get commercial investments from Shark Tank (India). As per the entrepreneur, the enterprise "got featured in Shark Tank (India) Season 1 and procured an all-sharks deal from the five maestros." They also received venture capital infusions from investors such as *Venture Catalyst, IA Growth Opportunities Fund-I,* and *Brew Opportunities Fund*. In the process, the enterprise was able to leverage 8.2 times the grants received from *the SAMRIDH* blended finance initiative.

The enterprise is focused on achieving cost efficiency by optimizing manufacturing through an advanced in-house research and development facility. Also, the cost of supplying to smaller towns and rural areas is subsidized by the concessional capital received from *SAMRIDH*.

This financial model combines elements of traditional product sales with innovative financing approaches and a focus on scalability and social impact. The enterprise's use of blended finance allows it to leverage various funding sources to support its growth and impact goals. The enterprise's transition from negative to positive EBITDA, along with significant revenue growth, suggests that their model is moving towards financial sustainability while maintaining their social mission.

The model appears designed to achieve rapid growth and market penetration while addressing a significant healthcare need. By leveraging initial grants and concessional funding to attract commercial investment and expand its product line and geographical reach, the enterprise aims to create a financially sustainable business that can also achieve significant social impact in healthcare accessibility.

4.3.3. Social Impact and Sustainable Development

The enterprise contributes to improving healthcare accessibility by developing a portable, affordable ECG device (Device) that can be used in remote and underserved areas. Example: The enterprise further plans to deploy the device in public health facilities nationwide, as well as in smaller towns, semi-urban areas, rural areas, and villages, making it accessible even in the most remote and underserved communities. At ₹7,200 ($85), the device is priced to be more affordable than traditional ECG machines.

The enterprise addresses critical emergency care needs through its portable pocket-ECG devices. This is significant, given that "less than 20% of hospitals in India have advanced equipment for detecting arrhythmia or coronary heart disease," as the entrepreneur stated. This makes it a life-saving technology that can prevent cardiovascular disease-related deaths through early detection. As per the entrepreneur, "Millions of lives lost to cardiovascular diseases may be prevented if round-the-clock monitoring equipment, routine monitoring, and cardiac evaluation are accessible."

The enterprise is expanding its impact beyond India to other countries, particularly in Africa. As reported by the entrepreneur, the enterprise has established its presence in 12 countries on the African subcontinent.

The enterprise is also engaged in strategic partnerships for greater impact. The enterprise collaborates with various stakeholders, including state governments, NGOs, and others, facilitating large-scale sales and penetration into the smaller towns and rural areas.

The enterprise's growth is creating employment opportunities and developing skills in the healthcare technology sector, thereby contributing to job creation and enhancing the healthcare workforce's skills. The enterprise's technology enables healthcare providers to offer better care, even in resource-constrained settings. One example shared by the entrepreneur was when a doctor from a non-profit, working in the interior villages of the Himalayan region, facing a potential cardiac emergency, used the pocket-ECG to confirm the condition and then "promptly directed the patients to the town hospital, where their (patient's) condition was confirmed based on the device reports, and they were admitted."

The enterprise's approach combines social impact with financial sustainability. The enterprise continues to innovate and expand its product line to address various healthcare needs. As reported by the entrepreneur, "*SAMRIDH's* support facilitated the enterprise to expand its product line of cardiac health products and services. These include the pocket-ECG, Military Grade Device, Device Neo, Device Pro, Device Legacy, and Alfa Test."

Regarding the Sustainable Development Goals, although not explicitly mentioned, the enterprise's work aligns with several SDGs, particularly SDG 3 (Good Health and Well-being) and SDG 10 (Reduced Inequalities).

The device is battery-free, potentially reducing electronic waste. The battery-free device provides instant, reliable reports on mobile phones.

In conclusion, the enterprise is addressing social impact and sustainable development by creating affordable, accessible healthcare technology that addresses a critical need in underserved communities. Their approach combines technological innovation with a sustainable business model, partnerships, and a focus on global expansion. By improving access to early cardiac diagnostics, the enterprise is not only saving lives but also advancing the broader goals of sustainable healthcare development.

4.3.4. Business and Financial Risks

The business and financial risks faced by the enterprise are discussed below, in the context of a manufacturing entity located in a small town and at a stabilized, mature early stage of its business.

4.3.4.1. Business Risks

There is a regulatory compliance risk as the enterprise must maintain CDSCO approval of its device. This is also linked to the quality assurance to maintain the device's incredible accuracy of 99.7 percent. The innovative technology that goes into maintaining this high level of accuracy is protected by patented technology, which needs protection from leakage of know-how and infringement, exposing the enterprise to intellectual property risk. As with any new technology, there is a risk that newer technologies will emerge, rendering the previous investment redundant and exposing the enterprise to technology obsolescence. Rapid advancements in medical technology may require continuous research and development investment.

The adoption of a new medical device by healthcare providers and patients may be challenging. This is also related to misinformation towards the new technology spread by existing market players, leading to competition risk.

The enterprise has expanded rapidly over the last two years, presenting operational challenges of organizational change and change management. This initial growth had been supported by a lot of strategic partnerships with *SAMRIDH*, seed funders, government and NGOs. This dependency on such partnerships for distribution and deployment may also pose financial risks if these partnerships falter.

4.3.4.2. Financial Risks

Reliance on various funding sources may create financial complexities, especially when trying to comply with the different fiduciary requirements for grants, loans and venture equity. In addition, entering new markets, especially internationally, incurs significant costs. International expansion also exposes the enterprise to currency fluctuations, especially from the volatile African markets. Operating in these overseas markets also requires maintaining regulatory compliance in these different countries. As per the entrepreneur, the enterprise "has registered Device ECG with the Kenya Pharmacy Board and is now working on registering the product in other African countries as well." Meeting regulatory requirements in multiple countries can be financially burdensome.

There is a cash flow management issue, as rapid expansion may strain cash resources. The enterprise had negative EBITDA until *SAMRIDH* funding came in, indicating potential cash flow issues. There is also additional pricing pressure because of the need to keep the product affordable. As the market penetration by the enterprise depends on strategic tie-ups and partnerships, the significant cost incurred in maintaining these partnerships also leads to cost pressures. In these circumstances, maintaining the 120% growth rate may be challenging and resource-intensive.

Significant research and development investment made by the enterprise since 2016 in highly accurate pocket-ECG devices may take time to recover, exposing them to investment recovery risk.

These risks highlight the complex challenges the enterprise faces in bringing an innovative medical device to market while maintaining affordability, quality, and global expansion. The enterprise's success will depend on effectively managing these risks through careful planning, robust quality control, strategic partnerships, and flexible financial management.

4.3.5. How Blended Finance Is Helping the Healthcare Social Enterprise

Blended finance is helping the enterprise address risks, financial sustainability, social impact, and sustainable development in several ways, as discussed below.

- **Addressing Risks:** The infusion of grants from the *SAMRIDH* blended finance initiative has enabled the enterprise to achieve self-sufficiency and foster innovation in cardiac health, as reported by the entrepreneur. This blended financing approach helps mitigate financial risks by overcoming the constraints in one type of funding by using the other type. For example, while grants reduce repayment liability, they do not guarantee funding over a longer period, as commercial investments do. As per the entrepreneur, *SAMRIDH* also provided business advisory and market access assistance to scale up the device. Such support helps validate the market potential, reducing market acceptance risk. *SAMRIDH* grants also helped the enterprise strengthen its technical and sales teams, thereby addressing operational risks associated with scaling.

- **Financial Sustainability:** Using concessional capital, the enterprise secured additional funding, achieving a leverage of approximately 8.2 times the grants. This additional cash infusion also supported 120% revenue growth and transitioned the enterprise from a negative EBIDTA of - ₹ 1,100,000 (-$13,253) to a positive EBIDTA of ₹ 2,800,000 ($ 33,700).
- **Social Impact:** The enterprise used concessional capital from *SAMRIDH* to extend the life-saving ECG technology to even the most underserved communities, transcending geographic and distribution-channel barriers and thus reaching underserved populations. This funding has allowed the enterprise to significantly scale its impact, with more than 1,500 ECG devices deployed and 63,000 patients screened. The enterprise also established its presence in 12 African countries.
- **Sustainable Development:** The concessional capital under the blended financing arrangement supports ongoing innovation and product development and augments healthcare services in smaller towns, semi-urban areas, rural areas, and villages. Beyond financial support, *SAMRIDH* also facilitated government linkages to expand the enterprise's reach, resulting in a significant increase in product visibility and demand. These partnerships, facilitated by blended finance, contribute to sustainable growth.
- **Enabling Innovation:** The blended finance, bringing in different kinds of grant, venture, and debt capital, helped expand product lines, including Military Grade Device, Device Neo, Device Pro, Device Legacy, and Alfa Test. Also, as told by the entrepreneur, "with this new capital, the enterprise is set for rapid expansion in India and globally, focusing on scaling its flagship innovation of the pocket-ECG device."

In conclusion, blended finance is crucial for the enterprise's development and deployment of innovative, affordable ECG technology. It provides the necessary capital to support research and development, operations, and expansion while allowing the enterprise to focus on its social impact goals. This approach enables the enterprise to address significant healthcare challenges in India and globally, balancing the need for financial sustainability with social impact and sustainable development.

The blended finance model helps de-risk the early stages of growth, making it more attractive for future commercial investments and supporting the long-term viability of the enterprise's mission to improve cardiac care accessibility. By combining philanthropic, public, and private capital, the enterprise can navigate the complex challenges of scaling a healthcare technology enterprise while maintaining its focus on serving underserved communities.

4.3.6. Conclusion

In conclusion, the innovative business model of the social enterprise, supported by blended finance, addresses critical healthcare needs while building a sustainable and scalable enterprise. The model balances risk management and financial sustainability with significant social impact and contribution to sustainable development.

4.4. Case Study 3: Primary Healthcare Enterprise

The third healthcare social enterprise studied was a primary healthcare enterprise, an early-stage enterprise based on an innovative, app-driven business model, to provide comprehensive primary healthcare services in a large metropolitan city in southern India. The enterprise was set up in 2016 by a young engineer and a doctor as a private limited company, and its financial statements are not publicly available; they are available only with the registrar of companies. The young engineer was moved by the lack of access to quality healthcare faced by her ailing father in a small town in the northeastern part of India. Hence, the enterprise was started with the mission of "transforming healthcare in India by providing high-quality, easily accessible primary care to the 'missing middle' population through affordable membership plans that cover doctor visits, treatments, and hospitalizations."

The enterprise is still in its early stages. Although revenue flows have started, it is yet to achieve positive EBIDTA. The business and financial model, sustainability and impact achieved, risks faced, and the role of blended finance in the enterprise are described in the following sections.

4.4.1. Business Model

The enterprise operates as India's first value-based, managed care enterprise. Their subscription-based model involves a subscription of ₹500 ($6) per month, against which the subscriber gets unlimited access to the enterprise's 360-degree OPD care. The subscription includes free diagnostics and prescription medicine, topped up with cashless health insurance. They have also aligned their incentives, with both fixed and variable pay. Variable pay depends on compliance with the laid-down treatment protocol and on how satisfied they are with the services, measured through customer rating and feedback.

The enterprise has established a network of 11 healthcare centers across the metropolitan city with the help of the grant funds received under the *SAMRIDH* blended finance initiative. There is also the option of a virtual connection, in addition to physical healthcare centres.

As per the entrepreneur interviewed, they "have built a technology platform through which they are standardizing the care that we are giving." The standardized protocol ensures the same treatment irrespective of which doctor is consulted in the network.

The enterprise focuses on blue-collar workers and their families. The entrepreneur said they prioritized the "gig workers" because they "lacked access to top-tier, protocol-based primary healthcare for themselves and their families." With a focus on gig workers and blue-collar workers, the enterprise has agreements with two industrial associations as its preferred primary healthcare providers.

The enterprise has a technology-driven approach. As per the entrepreneur, "We have built a technology platform through which we are standardizing the care that we are giving." They are using the technology platform to strengthen a prevention-focused model. The focus on prevention and management of health conditions is directed towards chronic diseases. The entrepreneur very clearly said that "once a chronic disease comes, it is not treatable. It is only manageable." Their protocol-based primary healthcare management platform has led to increased customer satisfaction. Five of their eleven health centers received a 5 out of 5 rating, and the rest received an average rating of 4.9.

The enterprise is also serious about cost optimization, not only for its own operations but also for its clients. The clients are prescribed mostly branded generics, which are WHO GMP-certified. This ensures that the medicine works and that the cost is reasonable for patients.

This business model aims to provide affordable, accessible, and high-quality healthcare to a traditionally underserved population while maintaining financial sustainability. It leverages technology, standardized protocols, and a network of care centers to deliver comprehensive primary care services. The model aligns incentives for patients, providers, and the enterprise itself, focusing on prevention and effective management of health conditions to reduce overall healthcare costs and improve outcomes.

4.4.2. Financial Model

The enterprise follows a subscription-based revenue model. They charge a subscription fee of ₹500 per month, in exchange for which clients receive unlimited access to the enterprise's "360-degree OPD care." This subscription model provides a steady, predictable revenue stream. There is also a health insurance top-up that covers hospitalization expenses. More than 10,000 people are enrolled in the insurance top-up, indicating the model is designed for scalability and can improve financial efficiency as it grows.

The enterprise has adopted a blended financing approach. They have received grant funding from the *SAMRIDH* blended finance initiative to the tune of ₹9,603,000 ($120,038). An additional grant of ₹5,000,000 ($60,000) has been obtained from the Indian government's Department of Science and Technology. These grants have been used to secure additional investments in the form of debt of ₹50,000,000 ($600,000) from Alteria Capital Funds and an equity infusion of ₹706,200,000 ($8.4 million) from MassMutual Ventures, Emphasis Fintech, and Times Internet. The blended financing enabled the enterprise to achieve a high leverage ratio of 50 times the grants mobilized. This indicates that the enterprise has been able to attract significant additional funding based on initial grant support.

The enterprise focuses on reducing the cost for its customers. They are optimizing the cost of medicines prescribed by using mostly branded generics, which are of the highest quality, and the cost is also lower than that of the branded medicines. This approach helps maintain affordability while ensuring quality. Also, the focus on primary healthcare is to reduce the overall cost of managed healthcare over time. This approach aims to reduce more expensive secondary and tertiary care needs. Moreover, the enterprise is trying to bring the health centers as close to clients as possible by operating a network of 11 healthcare centers across the metropolitan city. This indicates significant investment in physical infrastructure. They have also aligned the incentive payments to the treating doctors in their network, where, in addition to the fixed pay, they receive a variable component based on adherence to standardized treatment algorithms and customer feedback and ratings. This structure aims to balance quality care with cost management.

Guided by technology-driven efficiency, the enterprise has built a technology platform that is standardizing the care it provides. This results in operational efficiencies and cost savings, as reported by the entrepreneur.

The enterprise also engages in strategic partnerships for the client base. They have entered into agreements with two industrial associations in the suburbs of the metropolitan city. These partnerships reduce customer acquisition costs and provide a steady subscriber base.

This financial model combines traditional healthcare financing with innovative approaches such as blended finance and value-based care. It aims to create a sustainable enterprise while providing affordable healthcare to underserved populations. The high leverage ratio suggests that the initial grant funding has been effective in attracting significant additional investment, indicating investor confidence in their model.

The model's focus on primary care, technology-driven efficiency, and aligned incentives aims to control costs while improving health outcomes. This approach can potentially lead to long-term financial sustainability if it successfully reduces overall healthcare costs for its subscriber base.

4.4.3. Social Impact and Sustainable Development

The enterprise is very focused on increasing accessibility and affordability to quality, comprehensive healthcare for the lower-income segments of the population in cities and towns. The enterprise has established 11 healthcare centers across the metropolitan city. They also have agreements with industrial associations to acquire the blue-collar workers and gig workers as their customer base. In terms of affordability, the enterprise provides a health subscription for as low as ₹500 ($6) per month that covers all OPD expenses, including consultations, medicines, and diagnostics. This makes quality healthcare accessible to blue-collar workers and their families, who often struggle with healthcare costs. The subscription also includes unlimited access to the enterprise's "360-degree OPD care" through its state-of-the-art healthcare centers, along with the option to connect virtually and receive free diagnostics and prescription medicine while covered by cashless health insurance. The enterprise's focus on primary care also helps prevent unnecessary hospitalizations.

The enterprise uses standardized medical protocols to ensure high-quality care. This ensures consistent care irrespective of the treating doctor in the network. As per the entrepreneur, "it will be the same protocol, the same treatment that you are getting, the same prescription that you are getting." This is also in line with the principle of technology-driven healthcare.

Employment and Skill Development: The enterprise employs MBBS doctors, providing them with opportunities beyond traditional roles. This not only provides them employment but also builds their skill beyond their traditional clinical roles.

As a healthcare provider network, the enterprise addresses SDG-3 (Good Health and Well-being). In addition, by providing affordable private healthcare options, the enterprise helps reduce the burden on the overstretched public healthcare system. Hence, it also aligns well with government healthcare efforts.

The balancing of social impact and economic sustainability is summed up in this quote from the entrepreneur interviewed: "It is important that we do it profitably because that is how impact scales." This indicates their commitment to creating a model that is both impactful and financially sustainable, ensuring long-term viability and the potential to scale.

The interview and the reviewed documents also highlight the enterprise's focus on reaching underserved populations, with the entrepreneur stating, "For us, fulfillment is when we can reach Nagaon and make sure that we cover people there." This demonstrates their commitment to addressing healthcare disparities while maintaining a sustainable business model.

In conclusion, the enterprise's model addresses social impact by making quality healthcare more accessible and affordable for traditionally underserved populations. At the same time, its approach to sustainable development is to create a scalable, technology-driven model that aligns incentives to deliver better health outcomes while maintaining financial viability.

4.4.4. Business and Financial Risks

The business and financial risks faced by the enterprise are discussed below, given that it is a primary healthcare service provider, located in a large metropolitan city and in the early stages of its business (yet to register positive EBITDA).

4.4.4.1. Business Risks

As a new model of healthcare delivery, there is a risk that the target population (blue-collar workers) may not fully understand or adopt this approach. The entrepreneur's emphasis on aligning customer and service provider incentives suggests that the enterprise needs to ensure customer understanding and buy-in. Expanding the customer base from 11 healthcare centres to a larger population can pose operational challenges.

With a network of health facilities, maintaining consistent quality across all centres can be challenging as the network scales. This aligns with the enterprise's goal of ensuring the same treatment protocol, regardless of which centre or doctor a patient sees. Core to this quality control is its technology platform for standardizing care. This gives rise to a technology-dependence risk, as the enterprise relies heavily on the platform. Operating in the healthcare sector with an innovative model may also face regulatory scrutiny.

The enterprise also faces human resource risks, as attracting and retaining qualified MBBS doctors is challenging due to competitive employment options. This becomes all the more challenging as the enterprise aims to keep its prices low for the segment it is targeting, while it is forced to compensate doctors well and align their incentives with customer satisfaction and adherence to treatment protocols.

4.4.4.2. Financial Risks

The enterprise faces funding dependency risk, as it relies on multiple funding sources (grants, debt, equity), which creates its own complexities. Keeping costs low while maintaining quality can also be challenging, as the enterprise seeks to reduce costs through branded generics.

The subscription model of the business includes cashless health insurance. Providing cashless health insurance can lead to claim management challenges, thereby increasing insurance coverage risk.

The enterprise relies on partnerships with industrial associations to build its customer base. To ensure a captive market of blue-collar and gig workers, the enterprise depends on an agreement with two industrial associations. This exposes them to revenue concentration risk, and they need to widen their customer base in future.

The enterprise has made significant investments in physical healthcare centers and technology platforms. This exposes them to investment recovery risk as these investments in infrastructure and technology need to be recovered.

These risks highlight the complex landscape the enterprise navigates as it provides affordable, high-quality healthcare while building a sustainable business. The enterprise's innovative model, while addressing many healthcare challenges, also introduces unique risks that need careful management for long-term success.

4.4.5. How Blended Finance Is Helping the Healthcare Social Enterprise

Blended finance is helping the enterprise address various aspects of its business model, including risks, financial sustainability, social impact, and sustainable development, as explained below.

- **Addressing Risks:** The enterprise uses a mix of grant, debt, and equity funding, reducing dependence on a single source. For example, it has obtained *SAMRIDH* grants of ₹9,603,000 ($120,038). An additional grant of ₹5,000,000 ($60,000) has been obtained from the Indian government's Department of Science and Technology. These grants have been used to secure additional investments in the form of debt of ₹50,000,000 ($600,000) from Alteria Capital Funds and an equity infusion of ₹706,200,000 ($8.4 million) from MassMutual Ventures, Emphasis Fintech, and Times Internet. The grant components helped validate the model, reducing risk perception for subsequent investors. *SAMRIDH* grants also included support for commercial validation of the model, which is crucial for long-term financial sustainability.
- **Financial Sustainability:** The concessional capital (grants) enabled the enterprise to achieve a 50-times leverage on the grants, attracting substantial additional funding. The entrepreneur also mentioned that the partnership with *SAMRIDH* has facilitated the upcoming equity raise, showing how initial blended finance support can attract further investment. The blend of grants, debt, and equity enables the enterprise to optimize its capital structure for growth and sustainability.
- **Social Impact:** Blended finance enables the enterprise to provide affordable healthcare to blue-collar workers who often lack access to quality care. From just ₹500 ($6) per month, their subscribers get unlimited access to the enterprise's 360-degree OPD care. Not only does it ensure comprehensiveness of care, but the additional funding also allows the enterprise to expand its reach. For example, it already has more than 10,000 customers enrolled on insurance. The funding supports innovation by enabling the enterprise to manage its innovative care model. As per the entrepreneur

interviewed, "the enterprise operates as India's first value-based, managed care enterprise."

- **Sustainable Development:** By improving access to quality healthcare, the enterprise contributes to Sustainable Development Goal-3 (Good Health and Well-being). Example: While not explicitly mentioned, this is implied by their focus on providing affordable, quality healthcare.
- **Enabling Partnerships:** Blended finance has helped the enterprise on-board "three prominent industrial associations in the metropolitan city," expanding its reach and impact.
- **Supporting Innovation:** The mix of funding types allows the enterprise to innovate in its business model, combining primary care, insurance, and technology in a novel way for the Indian market. Example: "We have built a technology platform through which we are standardizing the care that we are giving."

4.4.6. Conclusion

In conclusion, blended finance is crucial for the enterprise, allowing it to balance financial sustainability with social impact. It provides the necessary capital to scale operations, invest in technology, and reach underserved populations, while also validating the model for commercial investors. This approach enables the enterprise to work towards sustainable healthcare development while building a viable business model that addresses the unique challenges of providing affordable, high-quality healthcare to blue-collar workers in India.

4.5. Case Study 4: Healthcare Enterprise

The fourth and final healthcare social enterprise studied was a hospital-and-outreach-services enterprise in a small north Indian town, a mature-stage enterprise. The enterprise began as a non-profit in 2001, providing primary healthcare services in remote villages across the hilly region around a small town in northern India. It was established by a doctor and a chartered accountant, with a pure philanthropic motive. But the couple quickly realized the need for a higher level of medical care, and in 2013, they established a for-profit hospital offering multi-speciality healthcare services. This case study focuses on the for-profit multi-speciality hospital as a social enterprise. The business and financial model, sustainability and impact achieved, risks faced, and the role of blended finance in the enterprise are described in the following sections.

4.5.1. Business Model

The enterprise offers a wide range of medical services, catering to diverse patient needs. The services include round-the-clock availability of a medical officer, internal medicine with ICU, Newborn and Child Care NICU, CT Scan, physiotherapy, Endoscopy, Colonoscopy, ERCP, round-the-clock emergency services, and ambulance services. It also offers a medicine store, online consultations, and digital financial transactions. The enterprise integrates various services under one roof, improving patient convenience and potentially reducing costs.

The enterprise conducts outreach activities in the higher mountainous region around the town through mobile medical units (MMUs) and five satellite centres. These programs extend healthcare access to remote and underserved areas.

The enterprise emphasizes providing equitable, affordable healthcare for all socio-economic groups. According to the entrepreneur interviewed, they are driven by the mission of providing "equitable and effective health service at an affordable price," covering patients from all sections of society, including "the elite, rich, slum dwellers and institutional staff," suggesting a broad patient base.

The enterprise is empaneled with various insurance providers, making its services accessible to insured patients. Example: The hospital is empaneled with *Ayushman Bharat*, ESI, CGHS, ECHS,

Golden Card, Star Health, Vipul Medical Corporation and all other private insurance and TPAs. The hospital also holds NABH accreditation, India's apex quality accreditation agency.

The enterprise has developed a "Center of Excellence" for respiratory care, focusing on COVID-19 and other respiratory illnesses. As per the entrepreneur, the center provides specialized respiratory care "with state-of-the-art ICU and HDU supported with a highly advanced diagnostic unit, headed by Pulmonologists, Physicians and Radiologists, with a Rehabilitation Unit for post-COVID complications, including a clinical psychologist."

The enterprise promotes gender inclusion within its organization and patient care. It not only devotes its resources to women's healthcare, both in the hospital and through outreach services, but the organization itself is run by a woman whose staff comprises 85% women.

In summary, the business model is a comprehensive, multispecialty hospital focused on providing affordable and accessible healthcare. They combine traditional hospital services with outreach programs and a Center of Excellence, leveraging blended financing to support their expansion and social impact goals. Their commitment to gender inclusivity further distinguishes their approach.

4.5.2. Financial Model

The enterprise utilizes a mix of funding sources, combining commercial capital with public and philanthropic funds. The *SAMRIDH* grants supported the enterprise in aggregating other funds through blended financing models and in setting up an integrated healthcare solution and rehabilitation facility for chronic respiratory diseases in Uttarakhand. The enterprise also mobilized additional funding from a bank in the form of debt of ₹29,000,000 ($400,000). The enterprise also relies on internal funds and promoter investments of approximately ₹40,000,000 Cr ($600,000). The enterprise has been able to leverage the grants received from *SAMRIDH* by 2.5 times.

The enterprise and multiple revenue streams: This includes service fees earned directly from patients for the multitude of healthcare services provided at the hospital. Outreach services at satellite clinics and MMUs are provided free of charge, with costs covered by philanthropic contributions from individuals and institutions. The hospital also gets insurance reimbursements from patients covered by different insurance programs. All this is done with a focus on providing affordable healthcare, implying efficient cost management. The enterprise plans to expand its services and reach, potentially leading to economies of scale.

The enterprise collaborates with government healthcare facilities, potentially sharing costs and resources through a public-private partnership. As per the entrepreneur interviewed, "the government CHC/PHC are provided communication and human resource assistance to integrate them with the outreach services."

The documents and information shared by the entrepreneur indicate that the enterprise is in a mature stage with steady revenue growth. Revenues increased 5% after *SAMRIDH's* support, from ₹115,100,000 ($1.39 million) to ₹120,600,000 ($1.43 million). There is also increased capital expenditure with investments in new facilities and equipment to enhance its service offerings. To meet these, the enterprise is considering additional funding of approximately $1 million to cover equipment and related working capital expenses.

This financial model combines elements of traditional healthcare financing with innovative approaches like blended finance. It aims to create a sustainable enterprise while providing affordable healthcare to a diverse population, including underserved communities. The model's focus on leveraging initial support, diversifying revenue streams, and improving profitability while expanding services and reach suggests a strategy aimed at long-term financial sustainability and social impact.

The use of blended finance and partnerships with government and non-profit organizations allows the enterprise to balance its social mission with financial viability, potentially enabling it to serve populations and areas that might not be commercially viable under a traditional private hospital model.

4.5.3. Social Impact and Sustainable Development

The enterprise provides equitable and affordable healthcare services to diverse socio-economic groups, catering to "the elite, rich, slum dwellers and institutional staff." This includes offering a wide range of healthcare services, demonstrating the comprehensive nature of the services. The enterprise is addressing critical healthcare needs as evidenced by developing the "center of excellence" on respiratory care, with state-of-the-art ICU and HDU facilities. The enterprise is also leveraging technology to provide healthcare in hard-to-reach areas by strengthening telemedicine and referral to the advanced respiratory care centre.

The enterprise promotes gender equality in its workforce and patient care. The enterprise provides additional support for its female employees, including daycare support, incentives, and basic upskilling. The enterprise offers targeted healthcare services for women. As the entrepreneur interviewed, "female patients are given specialized care and free of cost vitamins and minerals to help them maintain their general health."

The enterprise works to include marginalized populations in government healthcare programs. Their outreach services in the higher, mountainous regions integrate marginalized populations into government healthcare schemes, providing people with access to healthcare and promoting inclusiveness.

The enterprise aims to make healthcare more affordable by reducing associated expenses. According to the entrepreneur, satellite clinics and MMUs "make healthcare services more affordable by eliminating travel and accommodation expenses and providing specialist consultations free or at a nominal cost." This, coupled with high-end diagnostics, intensive care, and "center of excellence" status in their hospital, is also contributing to the development of healthcare infrastructure in underserved areas.

In conclusion, the enterprise is addressing social impact and sustainable development by providing affordable, accessible, and quality healthcare services to a diverse population, including underserved communities. Their approach combines traditional hospital services with innovative outreach programs, telemedicine, and specialized care centers. The enterprise's focus on gender inclusion, both in its workforce and patient care, further contributes to social development. By using a blended financing model and integrating with government schemes, the enterprise is working towards financial sustainability while maintaining its social mission. Their data-driven approach and focus on building healthcare infrastructure in underserved areas contribute to long-term sustainable development in the healthcare sector.

4.5.4. Business and Financial Risks

The business and financial risks faced by the enterprise are discussed below, given that it is a healthcare service provider, located in a small town and at a mature stage of its business.

4.5.4.1. Business Risks

As the enterprise relies heavily on revenue from insurance providers with which it is empaneled, it must comply with multiple regulatory standards.

Maintaining consistent quality across multiple services and satellite centers can be challenging, especially in difficult mountainous terrain and far-flung villages. Operating mobile medical units and satellite centers in remote areas may present logistical challenges.

Implementing and maintaining telemedicine services may pose technological challenges, especially regarding internet connectivity and bandwidth. There is also the risk of technology adoption among users and staff who may not be well-versed in the new technologies.

Attracting and retaining qualified medical professionals in remote areas can be difficult. The mobile units used for outreach services include a doctor, a pharmacist, a lab technician, a counselor, a nursing assistant, a data entry operator and support staff. Not having any one type of staff cripples the service delivery of the entire mobile unit. Hence, staffing risk is a big concern for the enterprise.

Although the entrepreneur describes the enterprise as "the best hospital with the best consultant physician" in the region, it also suggests that the enterprise faces competition from other healthcare providers.

Reliance on partnerships with government healthcare facilities may pose risks if these partnerships change or if the rapport with government officials and politicians changes.

4.5.4.2. Financial Risks

Reliance on blended financing and external funding sources may create financial vulnerabilities. Also, taking on additional debt for expansion can strain finances if not managed properly. Maintaining affordability while expanding services can pressure profit margins. Significant investments in new facilities and equipment may take time to yield returns. This may also affect the sustainability of growth. Maintaining growth and improving EBITDA margins may be challenging. However, the documents shared by the entrepreneur showed revenue growth of 5% and an improvement in EBITDA margin from 22% to 31% before and after *the SAMRIDH* grant support.

Expanding services and infrastructure while maintaining affordability may strain cash resources. Dependence on government schemes and insurance may lead to revenue fluctuations, especially in light of delayed payments. The entrepreneur did mention that, on average, 40% of the insurance payments are facing payment backlogs.

These risks highlight the complex challenges the enterprise faces in providing affordable, quality healthcare while maintaining financial sustainability and expanding its services.

4.5.5. How Blended Finance Is Helping the Healthcare Social Enterprise

Blended finance is helping the enterprise address risks, financial sustainability, social impact, and sustainable development in several ways, as discussed below.

- **Addressing Risks:** The *SAMRIDH* blended finance initiative supports the enterprise to aggregate funds using blended financing models, to set up an integrated healthcare solution and rehabilitation facility for chronic respiratory diseases in Uttarakhand. This approach helps mitigate financial risks by diversifying funding sources.
- **Leveraged Financing:** The financial support from *SAMRIDH* enables the enterprise to unlock additional debt funding from a bank to cover equipment and management expenses. Blended finance helps the enterprise acquire necessary equipment and manage operations, reducing operational risks. Blended finance attracts additional commercial investment, enhancing financial sustainability. Blended finance also helps address working capital needs, crucial for ongoing operations.
- **Social Impact:** The non-revenue-generating aspect of mobile units and satellite clinics, supported by concessional capital, increases accessibility of healthcare by bringing health services directly to underserved hilly areas through telemedicine and MMUs. Blended finance enables the enterprise to reach underserved populations. The concessional capital (grants) also makes healthcare services more affordable by eliminating travel and accommodation costs and providing specialist consultations at no cost or at a nominal cost. The funding

approach allows the enterprise to maintain affordability while expanding services.

- **Sustainable Development:** Blended finance supports the development of crucial healthcare infrastructure by providing non-returnable capital (grants) and also by helping leverage additional debt finance. It also enables integration with government programs through larger technical assistance provided by *SAMRIDH*, in addition to the capital.

Blended finance enables the enterprise to invest in innovative healthcare delivery that may not be sufficiently risky to finance through commercial investments. This included setting up of the "center of excellence" for respiratory care, outreach services through mobile units, telemedicine and online medical consultation. The blended finance approach supports the development of specialized care facilities.

Blended finance enables the scaling of impact through the grant-funded support for mobile units and satellite clinics. A total of 9,484 patients were served through MMUs, and 1,341 through Satellite Centres in 2023.

4.5.6. Conclusion

In conclusion, blended finance is crucial for the enterprise's development and expansion of healthcare services, particularly in underserved areas. It provides the capital needed to support infrastructure development, operational expenses, and innovative healthcare delivery methods, while allowing the hospital to focus on its social impact goals. This approach enables the enterprise to address significant healthcare challenges in Uttarakhand, balancing the need for financial sustainability with social impact and sustainable development.

The blended finance model helps de-risk the expansion and growth stages, making it more attractive to future commercial investors and supporting the hospital's long-term mission to provide affordable, accessible healthcare. By combining philanthropic, public, and private capital, the enterprise can navigate the complex challenges of scaling a healthcare facility while maintaining its focus on serving diverse communities, including marginalized populations.

4.6. How Healthcare Social Enterprises Address Social Impact and Business Viability

There are certain key considerations that drive a social enterprise. Using the interview responses and documents shared by the entrepreneurs, key considerations were identified using a word cloud that shows the keywords, with the size of each word representing its frequency in the text. The word cloud thus obtained is shown in figure 4.2 below.

Figure 4.2: Word Cloud of Key Words Mentioned by the Social Entrepreneurs

As the word cloud above clearly shows, the most important consideration for the healthcare social enterprises covered in the research is cost, followed by affordability and quality. As social enterprises targeting the bottom-of-the-pyramid population segment, affordability seems to be their main lever for achieving the social impact. But the dominance of cost considerations hints at economic viability as their primary objective. Quality concern also seems to be related to both cost and affordability. As social enterprises, these enterprises address their core mission of achieving impact by ensuring the affordability of the products and services they offer. But to ensure these remain affordable without affecting business bottom lines, the enterprises have to ensure low cost. Hence, the overwhelming concern for cost, followed by affordability, irrespective of the stage of business, location or type of business.

Growth and risk also figure as issues of some concern, but way below in priority as compared to cost, affordability and quality. A few entrepreneurs also mentioned, once or twice, issues of equity, finance, sustainability, "small towns," and blended finance.

With the understanding that the healthcare social enterprises in the Indian context are more worried about cost, affordability and quality, the key features of their business model were analyzed, as shown in table 4.1 below.

	High-end equipment manufacturer	**Portable equipment manufacturer**	**Primary care clinic**	**Hospital + outreach services**
Business-to-business (B2B) sales	√	√	---	---
Business-to-consumer (B2C) sales	---	√	√	√
Center of Excellence	---	---	---	√
Computer assisted protocol-based care	---	---	√	---
Cost effective manufacturing and service delivery	√	---	√	√
Demand side financing/health insurance	---	---	---	√
Geographic focus	√	---	---	---
Global expansion	---	√	---	---
Healthcare service provisioning	---	√	√	√
Multi-specialty	---	---	---	√

healthcare				
Networked care model	---	---	√	---
Outpatient and primary health care	---	---	√	---
Outreach healthcare services in far-flung areas	---	---	---	√
Partnerships for leveraging their value-chain	√	√	√	---
Patented product	√	---	---	---
Phased market entry	√	---	---	---
Priority population focus	---	---	√	√
Product development and innovation	√	√	---	---
Product sales and distribution	---	√	---	---
Quality rating for value proposition	---	---	√	---
Social impact focus	√	√	√	√
Technology differentiation	√	---	---	---
Value-based managed healthcare	---	---	√	---
Virtual connectivity for healthcare	---	---	√	---

Table 4.1: Business Model of Healthcare Social Enterprises

As shown in the table above, no feature is common to all four types of healthcare social enterprises. But most of them directly reach out to consumers using the B2C mode. In addition, most of them have a focus on cost-effective manufacturing and service delivery. This suggests that they prioritize providing affordable healthcare solutions to their customers. Also, most of the healthcare social enterprises have partnerships for leveraging their value chain. This indicates that they recognize the importance of collaborations and strategic partnerships in achieving their goals. Further, most of the healthcare social enterprises have a priority population focus. This means that they have identified specific target populations that they aim to serve, and their business models are designed to meet the needs of these populations. Lastly, most of the healthcare social enterprises have a social impact focus. This suggests that they are driven by a desire to make a positive impact on society, rather than solely by profit motives.

Looking at the unique features of the business model, the high-end equipment manufacturer has a patented product, which indicates that it has developed a unique and innovative solution that is protected by intellectual property rights. They also have a phased market-entry approach, unlike the other types of social enterprises studied. The enterprise has technology differentiation, meaning it has developed advanced technologies that set it apart from competitors.

The unique features of portable equipment manufacturers include a global expansion strategy, indicating they aim to expand their operations and reach new markets worldwide. The Portable equipment manufacturer also has a unique focus on product sales and distribution, indicating a well-established network for getting its products to market.

A unique feature of the primary care clinic is computer-assisted, protocol-based healthcare, aimed at standardizing care across all clinics and doctors. It has a networked care model, which means it takes a collaborative approach to care, working with other healthcare providers and organizations. The enterprise has uniquely integrated quality ratings into its value proposition. It also has a value-based managed healthcare approach, which means that it focuses on delivering high-quality care that is tailored to the needs of its patients. The primary care clinic also offers virtual care, indicating that it uses digital technologies to connect with patients and deliver care remotely.

Coming to the fourth type of healthcare social enterprise, the unique feature of the "hospital + outreach services" model is its "center of excellence" which suggests that it has a specialized facility or team that is dedicated to delivering high-quality healthcare services. Its business model also includes multi-speciality healthcare services, suggesting it offers a broad range of medical specialities and services to its patients. In addition, it provides outreach healthcare services in far-flung areas, which indicates that it is committed to delivering care to underserved and remote populations.

Thus, it is evident that the business models of healthcare social enterprises share several common features, including a focus on cost-effective manufacturing and service delivery, partnerships to leverage their value chains, a population-focused priority, and a social impact focus. However, each type of healthcare social enterprise also has unique features that distinguish it from the others. The high-end equipment manufacturer focuses on technology differentiation and global expansion, while the portable equipment manufacturer focuses on product development and innovation. The primary care clinic focuses on outpatient and primary health care, while the "hospital + outreach services" model focuses on multi-speciality healthcare and outreach services in far-flung areas. By understanding these common and unique features, healthcare social enterprises can develop effective business models that meet the needs of their customers and drive positive social impact.

Next, we look at the features of the financial models of the healthcare social enterprises studied. This is enumerated in table 4.2 below.

	High-end Equipment Manufacturer	Portable Equipment Manufacturer	Primary Care Clinic	Hospital + Outreach Services
Affordable pricing	√	√	√	√
Cost optimization	√	√	√	√
Cost-effective manufacturing	√	√	---	---
Designed for scale up and growth	---	√	√	√
Grants with equity infusion and venture funding	---	√	√	√
Incentive alignment for healthcare providers	---	---	√	---
Integrated with demand side financing	---	---	√	---
Investment in infrastructure	---	---	√	√
Leveraged financing	√	√	√	√
Long term cost savings for customers	√	---	√	---
Multiple revenue streams	---	---	---	√
One-time payment for product/service	---	√	---	√
Pay-as-you-use model	√	---	---	
Public-private partnership	---	---	---	√
Recoverable grants	√	---	---	---
Subscription-based payment model	---	---	√	---
Technology driven efficiency	---	---	√	---

Table 4.2: Financial Model of Healthcare Social Enterprises

It is evident that there are several features that are common to all four types of healthcare social enterprises. All four types of healthcare social enterprises focus on cost optimization, prioritizing cost reduction and operational efficiency. All of them have access to grants with equity infusions and venture funding, suggesting a strong network of investors and funding sources. Finally, all four types of healthcare social enterprises have leveraged financing, meaning they use debt or other financing to fund their operations and growth.

But there are some unique features of the financial model, specific to the social enterprises. Starting with the high-end equipment manufacturer, it offers a pay-as-you-use model, meaning customers only pay for the products and services they use. It has access to unique recoverable grants, which are zero-interest, non-legal-obligation funds with repayment only "desirable" and helpful for building credit history.

The unique feature of the financial model of the primary healthcare clinic is the alignment of doctors' incentive payments, suggesting that it prioritizes aligning its healthcare providers' incentives with its patients' needs. Their model integrates demand-side financing, enabling it to understand its patients' financing needs and provide tailored solutions. The enterprise uses a subscription-based payment model, meaning customers pay a recurring fee for access to its products and services. They have also adopted technology-driven efficiency, which suggests that it prioritizes using technology to improve the efficiency and effectiveness of its operations.

Coming to the "hospital + outreach" enterprise, its unique financial model includes multiple revenue streams, indicating that it has diversified its income sources to reduce dependence on a single source. The enterprise also has a public-private partnership, indicating that it has collaborated with government or other public-sector organizations to deliver its products and services.

The financial models of healthcare social enterprises share several common features, including a focus on cost optimization, multiple revenue streams, leveraged financing, and long-term cost savings for customers. However, each type of healthcare social enterprise also has unique features that distinguish it from the others. By understanding these common and unique features, healthcare social enterprises can develop effective financial models that meet the needs of their customers and drive positive social impact.

Having examined the features of the business and financial models of the healthcare social enterprises studied, we now examine how they fulfill their primary purpose: achieving social outcomes and impact. Different ways in which healthcare social enterprises address social impact and sustainability are listed in table 4.3 below.

	High-end Equipment Manufacturer	**Portable Equipment Manufacturer**	**Primary Care Clinic**	**Hospital + Outreach Services**
Addressing healthcare gaps and critical needs	√	√	√	√
Affordable products/services	√	√	√	√
Alignment with government initiatives	√	---	√	√
Alignment with Sustainable Development Goals	---	√	√	---
Comprehensive healthcare	---	---	√	---
Demand side financing/health insurance	---	---	√	---
Empowering healthcare providers	---	√	---	---
Environmentally sustainable technology	√	√	---	---
Expanding healthcare infrastructure	√	---	√	√

Focus on priority geographies and populations	√	√	√	√
Global reach	---	√	---	---
Improved access to products/services	√	√	√	√
Improved quality	√	---	√	---
Innovation for social good	---	√	---	---
Lifesaving technology	---	√	---	---
Localization and job creation	√	√	√	---
Partnerships for accelerated social impact	---	√	---	---
Reducing associated healthcare costs	√	---	---	√
Reducing dependency on imports	√	---	---	---
Sustainable business model	---	√	---	---
Technology-driven healthcare	---	---	√	√

Table 4.3: How Healthcare Social Enterprises Address Social Impact and Sustainability

There are several features of addressing social impact and sustainability that are common to all four types of healthcare social enterprises. These include a focus on addressing healthcare gaps and critical needs, suggesting they prioritize delivering essential healthcare services to underserved populations. All four types of healthcare social enterprises offer affordable products and services, indicating that they prioritize making healthcare accessible to a wide range of customers. All the social enterprises studied focus on priority geographies and populations, meaning they prioritize delivering healthcare services to regions and populations in greatest need. They also look at improved access to products and services, indicating that it prioritizes making its products and services accessible to a wide range of customers.

Looking at the unique ways healthcare social enterprises address social impact and sustainability, the high-end equipment manufacturer focuses on reducing its reliance on imports, suggesting it prioritizes developing local solutions and reducing dependence on imported products and services. On the other hand, the portable equipment manufacturer focuses on empowering healthcare providers by prioritizing their support and enabling them to deliver high-quality care. They prioritize innovation for social good, developing new solutions to address social and environmental challenges. The portable equipment manufacturer has lifesaving technology, indicating that it develops products and services with the potential to save lives. They have also uniquely forged partnerships to accelerate social impact, suggesting that they prioritize collaborating with other organizations to deliver healthcare services and programs. Lastly, the portable equipment manufacturer has a sustainable business model, which suggests that it prioritizes developing a business model that is financially sustainable and environmentally responsible.

Among healthcare service providers, the primary care clinic's unique approach to social impact and sustainability is to provide comprehensive healthcare, suggesting it prioritizes delivering a broad range of services to its customers. They have also uniquely adopted demand-side financing and health insurance, prioritizing customer access to healthcare services through financing and insurance options. The "hospital + outreach" enterprise does not have any unique feature observed or reported.

How healthcare social enterprises address social impact and sustainability share several common features, including addressing healthcare gaps and critical needs, offering affordable products and services, aligning with government initiatives, and focusing on priority geographies and populations. By understanding these common and unique features, healthcare social enterprises can develop effective strategies to address social impact and sustainability, and to deliver high-quality healthcare services to their customers.

4.7. Risks Faced by Healthcare Social Enterprises

As discussed earlier in the literature review section, social enterprises face unique risks, including both business and financial risks. The risks mentioned by the entrepreneurs interviewed are listed in table 4.4 below.

	High-end Equipment Manufacturer	**Portable Equipment Manufacturer**	**Primary Care Clinic**	**Hospital + Outreach Services**
Business Risks				
Competition risk	√	√	---	√
Dependency on partnerships	√	√	---	√
Intellectual property theft risk	√	√	---	---
Market acceptance risk	√	√	√	---
Operational risk in remote areas	---	---	---	√
Quality control risk	---	√	√	√
Regulatory risks	√	√	√	√
Retention risk of qualified professionals	---	---	√	√
Scaling up risk	√	√	√	---
Technological dependence and obsolescence risk	---	√	√	---
Technology risks	√	---	---	√
Financial Risks				

Affordable pricing negatively affecting profits	√	√	---	---
Cost management risk	√	---	√	√
Currency fluctuation risk	---	√	---	
Debt management risk	---	---	---	√
Dependence on grants and concessional capital	√	√	√	√
Foreign exchange risk	√	---	---	---
High leverage risk	√	---	---	---
High market penetration costs	---	√	---	---
High regulatory compliance costs	---	√	---	---
Long recovery time for investments on infrastructure, research and development	√	√	√	√
Revenue uncertainties	√	√	√	√
Risk in sustaining high growth	---	√	---	√
Risk of refusal by health insurance providers	---	---	√	---

Table 4.4: Risks Faced by Healthcare Social Enterprises

As shown in the table above, most business risks are common across all four types of healthcare social enterprises studied, but many financial risks are unique to each enterprise. Among business risks, all four types of healthcare social enterprises face regulatory risks that require them to comply with laws and regulations governing the healthcare industry. Looking at financial risks, all four types of enterprises face the risk of dependence on grants and concessional capital, meaning they may rely on external funding sources such as grants, loans, or equity investments to support their operations and growth. They also face the risk of long recovery times for infrastructure and research and development investments, suggesting these investments may require significant upfront costs and take time to generate returns. Also, all four types of healthcare social enterprises face revenue uncertainties, which may lead to fluctuations in revenue driven by changes in demand, pricing, or reimbursement rates.

Given the unique risks enterprises face, the high-end equipment manufacturer faces foreign exchange risk because it relies on many imported components for its products. They also face high leverage risk, indicating they may have high levels of debt or financial leverage that can increase their risk of default or financial distress. On the other hand, the portable equipment manufacturer must deal with high market penetration and regulatory compliance costs.

The primary care clinic faces the risk of refusal by health insurance providers, which may make it difficult to obtain reimbursement for its services. The "hospital + outreach services" enterprise faces operational risks in remote areas, which may make it difficult to deliver healthcare services due to limited infrastructure, transportation, or staffing.

The different business and financial risks faced by healthcare social enterprises share several common features, including competition risk, regulatory risks, revenue uncertainties, and retention risk of qualified professionals. By understanding these common and unique features, healthcare social enterprises can develop effective risk management strategies to mitigate these risks and ensure their long-term sustainability and success.

4.8. How Blended Finance Enables Healthcare Social Enterprises to Address Risks and Social Impact

Having reviewed the business and financial models of the four types of healthcare social enterprises and the risks they face, we next examine how blended finance helps them address these risks. Table 4.5 below lists how blended finance enables the healthcare social enterprise to address different risks and social impact.

	High-end Equipment Manufacturer	**Portable Equipment Manufacturer**	**Primary Care Clinic**	**Hospital + Outreach Services**
Financial Risk				
Financial risk mitigation and funding diversification	√	√	√	√
Leverage for additional funding	√	√	√	√
Subsidization for affordability	√	---	---	√
Transition to profitability	---	√	---	---
Operational Risk				
Adherence to environmental considerations	√	---	---	---
Enabling innovation	√	√	√	√
Building strategic partnerships	√	√	√	
Long-term capacity building	---	---	---	√
Support in obtaining patents and	√	---	---	---

clearances				
Support in reducing operational cost burden	√	√	---	√
Market Risk				
Global reach	---	√	---	---
Market expansion support	---	√	---	---
Phased development support	√	---	---	---
Product and market validation support	√	√	√	---
Revenue growth	---	√	---	---
Social Impact				
Addressing healthcare service and infrastructure gaps	√	√		√
Aligning with Sustainable Development Goals	√	---	√	---
Assistance in reaching out to priority geographies and population segments	√	---	√	---
Improving healthcare access	√	√		√
Scaling up support for impact	√	√	√	√

Table 4.5: How Blended Finance Enables the Healthcare Social Enterprise to Address Risks and Social Impact

It is evident from the above table that there are several features that are common to all four types of healthcare social enterprises. All four types of healthcare social enterprises use blended finance to mitigate financial risks and diversify their funding sources, suggesting they prioritize financial risk management and a stable financial foundation. Related to this is the use of blended finance to leverage additional funding by all the healthcare social enterprises, indicating that they prioritize accessing new funding sources to support their growth and development. They also use blended finance for innovation, suggesting that it helps develop new products and services that address specific healthcare needs. All four types of healthcare social enterprises use blended finance to subsidize their products and services, making them more affordable for their customers, which suggests that they prioritize delivering affordable healthcare solutions. Finally, blended finance is used by these enterprises to support scaling up their impact.

There are also two other ways in which blended finance helps social enterprises, as observed in the case of three of the four enterprises studied. These include support for building strategic partnerships, indicating a prioritization of collaborating with other organizations to deliver its products and services. These enterprises also use blended finance to support product and market validation, enabling them to test and validate their products and services across different markets and customer segments.

On the other hand, each type of healthcare social enterprise also has unique features that distinguish it from the others. The high-end equipment manufacturer uses blended finance to support patent and clearance applications, thereby protecting its intellectual property and ensuring regulatory compliance. It also uses blended finance for phased development and market entry.

The portable equipment manufacturer uses blended finance to transition to profitability, which means that they prioritize achieving financial sustainability and long-term viability. They also use blended finance to support revenue growth, suggesting they prioritize revenue growth and financial sustainability.

For healthcare service provider enterprises, there were few unique uses of blended, except for the "hospital + outreach services" enterprise, which used it for long-term capacity building, in line with its focus on internal capabilities and capacity to deliver high-quality products and services.

Having looked at the role of blended finance in addressing financial, operational, and market risks while enabling health care social enterprises to address social impact, it is important to examine whether this varies across the dimensions of the social enterprises. These dimensions examine the role of blended finance in the context of the enterprises' geographic location, whether they are manufacturing or service providers, and whether they are in the early or mature stages of their business.

The different ways blended finance plays out in addressing risks and social impact for social enterprises located in big cities, as opposed to those in small towns, are outlined in table 4.6 below.

	SE-Big City	**SE-Small City**
Financial Risk		
Financial risk mitigation and funding diversification	√	√
Leverage for additional funding	√	---
Subsidization for affordability	√	√
Transition to profitability	---	√
Operational Risk		
Adherence to environmental considerations	√	---
Enabling innovation	√	√
Building strategic partnerships	√	√
Long-term capacity building	---	√
Support in obtaining patents and clearances	√	---
Support in reducing operational cost burden	√	√
Market Risk		
Global reach	√	√
Market expansion support	---	√
Phased development support	√	---
Product and market validation support	√	√
Revenue growth	---	√

Social Impact		
Addressing healthcare service and infrastructure gaps	√	√
Aligning with Sustainable Development Goals	√	---
Assistance in reaching out to priority geographies and population segments	√	---
Improving healthcare access	√	√
Scaling up support for impact	√	√

Table 4.6: How Blended Finance Works for Healthcare Social Enterprises in Big and Small Cities

As shown in the table above, the ways in which blended finance enables social enterprises to address different risks and achieve social impact are very similar across big cities and small towns. But there are some differences observed. Healthcare social enterprises in big cities tend to use blended finance to leverage additional funding, support adherence to environmental considerations, obtain patents and clearances, plan a phased business development, reach priority geographies and population segments, and align with the SDGs. On the other hand, enterprises in smaller towns tend to use blended finance to transition to profitability, build long-term capacity, expand markets, and grow revenue. Over ten of the twenty listed uses of blended finance are the same for enterprises in big cities as in small towns.

Next, we look at the different ways blended finance can work for manufacturing and healthcare service providers, as shown in table 4.7 below.

	Manufacturer	**Service Provider**
Financial Risk		
Financial risk mitigation and funding diversification	√	√
Leverage for additional funding	√	√
Subsidization for affordability	√	√
Transition to profitability	√	---

Operational Risk		
Adherence to environmental considerations	√	---
Enabling innovation	√	√
Building strategic partnerships	√	√
Long-term capacity building	---	√
Support in obtaining patents and clearances	√	---
Support in reducing operational cost burden	√	√
Market Risk		
Global reach	√	---
Market expansion support	√	---
Phased development support	√	---
Product and market validation support	√	√
Revenue growth	√	---
Social Impact		
Addressing healthcare service and infrastructure gaps	√	√
Aligning with Sustainable Development Goals	√	√
Assistance in reaching out to priority geographies and population segments	√	√
Improving healthcare access	√	√
Scaling up support for impact	√	√

Table 4.7: How Blended Finance Works for Manufacturing and Healthcare Service Providers

As shown in the table above, manufacturing entities and healthcare service providers use blended finance to address risks and social impact in very similar ways. Eleven of the twenty listed uses of blended finance are similar across both types of social enterprises. Also, there is no difference in the way blended finance is used to address social impact by manufacturers and healthcare service providers. Also, the uses of blended finance to address financial risks are mostly similar across the two types of enterprises. However, the use of blended finance to address market risks is predominantly undertaken by manufacturing enterprises.

Lastly, we examine the different ways blended finance is used by early- and mature-stage social enterprises. This is shown in table 4.8 below.

	Early-Stage SE	Matured Stage SE
Financial Risk		
Financial risk mitigation and funding diversification	√	√
Leverage for additional funding	√	√
Subsidization for affordability	√	√
Transition to profitability	---	√
Operational Risk		
Adherence to environmental considerations	√	---
Enabling innovation	√	√
Building strategic partnerships	√	√
Long-term capacity building	---	√
Support in obtaining patents and clearances	√	---
Support in reducing operational cost burden	√	√
Market Risk		
Global reach	---	√
Market expansion support	---	√
Phased development support	√	---
Product and market validation support	√	√
Revenue growth	---	√
Social Impact		
Addressing healthcare service and infrastructure gaps	√	√
Aligning with Sustainable Development Goals	√	---
Assistance in reaching out to priority geographies and population segments	√	---
Improving healthcare access	√	√
Scaling up support for impact	√	√

Table 4.8: How Blended Finance Works for Healthcare Social Enterprises at Early and Mature Stages of Business

As seen in the table above, early-stage healthcare social enterprises use blended finance exclusively to ensure adherence to environmental conditions, support patent and clearance applications, facilitate phased business growth, align with the SDGs, and expand outreach to priority geographies. Whereas, mature-stage enterprises make exclusive use of blended finance for transitioning to profitability, long-term capacity building, expanding global reach and markets, and enabling revenue growth.

This is clearly evident from the above tables that geographic location, type of enterprise (manufacturing versus service delivery), and stage of business explain some of the differences in the use of blended finance to address risks and social impact, but there are many common traits across these background differences. Also, it is evident that social enterprises need much more support from blended finance than just access to capital, primarily in the form of technical assistance and business advisory services.

4.9. Conceptual Model: Blended Finance and its Role in Addressing Risks and Social Impact for Healthcare Social Enterprises

A conceptual model is developed based on the four case studies and a detailed analysis of how the studied healthcare social enterprises used blended finance to mitigate business and financial risks while addressing social impact. This is a suggested framework emerging from this study and will need further testing in future research with a larger sample of social enterprises from health and other social sectors. The conceptual model is shown in figure 4.3 below.

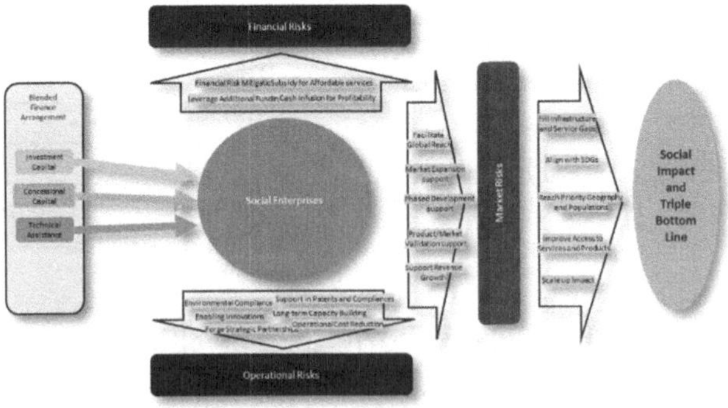

Figure 4.3: Conceptual Model of Blended Finance and Its Role in Addressing Risks and Social Impact for Healthcare Social Enterprises

As shown in the conceptual model above, blended finance includes concessional capital, investment capital, and technical assistance. The social enterprises receive these three inputs from blended finance arrangements to address financial risks and operational and market risk components of the overall business risk. While addressing these risks, the social enterprises also undertake additional interventions to achieve social impact and the triple bottom line.

The suggested model also highlights which particular strategies and interventions for risk reduction and impact are supported by which component of blended finance. Based on case studies, in-depth interviews with entrepreneurs, and other shared documents, it emerges that concessional capital subsidized affordable services and provided cash infusions to SEs to address financial risks. In addition, it finances innovations to address operational risks and helps SEs reach priority geographies, thereby improving access to enterprises' products and services. The commercial capital portion of blended finance supports financial risk mitigation. It does not seem to play a role in operational risk mitigation, but it supports market expansion and phased development to address market risks faced by the SEs, thereby enabling scaling up impact. Investment capital finances the filling of infrastructure and service gaps while also supporting the scaling-up efforts.

The most important revelation of the study is that the softer part of blended finance is supported through technical assistance. This seems to help the SEs address operational risk by supporting efforts to ensure environmental compliance, obtain patient and other compliance certifications, build long-term capacity, forge strategic partnerships, and reduce operational costs. To address financial risks, technical assistance helps with leveraging additional funding from other sources. It also facilitates global reach for addressing market risks. Finally, technical assistance helps SEs align with the Sustainable Development Goals to achieve greater sustainability impact.

4.10. Summary of Findings

The four case studies show that each enterprise has developed innovative approaches to address healthcare challenges. Whether through technology (MRI and ECG devices), service delivery (subscription-based primary care), or hybrid models (hospital with outreach services), innovation is central to their success.

Blended finance emerges as a crucial enabler for healthcare social enterprises. It helps mitigate early-stage risks, attract commercial capital, support innovation and R&D, enable market expansion, and maintain affordability while building financial sustainability.

All enterprises prioritize making healthcare more accessible and affordable, though their approaches vary by context and target population. Also, technology plays a vital role across all cases, whether in product development, service delivery, or operational efficiency. It is also evident that almost all enterprises leverage partnerships with various stakeholders, including government agencies, private-sector players, and international organizations.

The financial risks faced by the healthcare social enterprises studied include their dependence on grants and external funding, the need for significant capital investment, long investment recovery periods, and revenue uncertainties. Operational risks faced by these enterprises are maintaining quality across locations, attracting and retaining qualified professionals, managing technology dependencies and operating in remote areas. These social enterprises face market risks, including competition from established players, market acceptance of new models, regulatory compliance requirements, and challenges in scaling up their businesses.

The study reveals significant differences between enterprises in big cities and those in small towns. The social enterprises located in bigger cities have better access to funding and resources, a more competitive environment, a larger potential market and higher operating costs. In contrast, the enterprises in smaller towns have a greater focus on basic healthcare needs, a more challenging operating environment, stronger community connections and lower operating costs.

Blended finance emerges as a crucial tool for healthcare social enterprises, serving multiple purposes. Blended finance plays a risk-mitigation role by reducing early-stage risks, enabling innovation and experimentation, and supporting market validation. Blended finance helps scale up and grow social enterprises by attracting commercial capital, enabling infrastructure development, and supporting market expansion. It facilitates achieving social impact by maintaining affordability, encouraging outreach to underserved populations, and supporting quality improvement. It also plays a significant role in future sustainability by establishing a pathway to financial sustainability, enabling technology adoption, and supporting internal capacity-building for the supported social enterprises.

4.11. Conclusion

The study of these four healthcare social enterprises provides valuable insights into how social enterprises can effectively address healthcare challenges in India. The cases demonstrate that successful healthcare social enterprises combine innovative business models, strategic use of blended finance, strong focus on accessibility and affordability, effective use of technology and strategic partnerships.

The role of blended finance is particularly crucial in enabling these enterprises to balance their social impact goals with financial sustainability. It provides the necessary support for innovation and risk-taking while building pathways to commercial viability.

The findings suggest that supporting healthcare social enterprises through blended finance and other enabling mechanisms can significantly improve access to and quality of healthcare in India. However, support needs to be tailored to the specific context and needs of different types of enterprises, taking into account factors such as location, business model, and stage of development.

The success of these enterprises suggests several implications for policy and practice. There is a need for expanded blended finance mechanisms. It is essential to have tailored support based on enterprise type and location. The role of technology in enabling new healthcare delivery models has also been highlighted through these case studies. All these need building ecosystems that support social enterprises. These insights can inform the development of more effective support mechanisms for social enterprises in general and healthcare social enterprises in particular, ultimately contributing to improved triple bottom line environmental, social, and economic sustainability in the context of low- and middle-income countries like India.

Chapter 5 | Discussion

5.1. Discussion of Results

The study of these four healthcare social enterprises provides valuable insights into how social enterprises can effectively address healthcare challenges in India. The cases demonstrate that successful healthcare social enterprises combine innovative business models, strategic use of blended finance, strong focus on accessibility and affordability, effective use of technology and strategic partnerships.

Blended finance emerges as a crucial tool for healthcare social enterprises, serving multiple purposes. Blended finance plays a risk-mitigation role by reducing early-stage risks, enabling innovation and experimentation, and supporting market validation. Blended finance helps scale up and grow social enterprises by attracting commercial capital, enabling infrastructure development, and supporting market expansion. It facilitates achieving social impact by maintaining affordability, encouraging outreach to underserved populations, and supporting quality improvement. It also plays a significant role in future sustainability by establishing a pathway to financial sustainability, enabling technology adoption, and supporting internal capacity-building for the supported social enterprises.

The following sections discuss how the study findings compare with existing literature on the topic of social enterprises and the use of blended finance by such enterprises. These discussions identify specific aspects of risk mitigation and social impact that are not adequately covered in the existing literature, as addressed by social enterprises. Based on the discussion, an emerging conceptual model is also suggested that shows how healthcare social enterprises use blended finance to address business and financial risks, as well as social impact and business viability.

5.2. How Healthcare Social Enterprises Address Social Impact and Business Viability

Social enterprises have emerged as crucial players in addressing societal challenges while maintaining business sustainability. This discussion covers how social enterprises, particularly in healthcare, address social impact, business risks, financial risks, and business viability, drawing from both theoretical literature and practical case studies.

From the section on literature review, we see that "social entrepreneurship can stimulate ideas for more socially acceptable and sustainable business strategies" (Seelos & Mair, 2005). The literature emphasizes that social enterprises aim to "create economic opportunities while simultaneously operating with reference to the financial bottom-line" (Emerson & Twersky, 1996). The study findings support this assertion, showing that healthcare social enterprises address social impact and sustainability by addressing healthcare gaps and critical needs, providing affordable products and services, aligning with government initiatives, and focusing on priority geographies and populations.

The findings from the case studies and analysis reveal several concrete approaches. The social enterprises are found to be technology-driven for achieving impact. For example, the social enterprises covered in this study are engaged in developing affordable MRI technology, portable ECG devices for remote areas, digital health platforms for standardized care, and telemedicine solutions to improve accessibility. There are also service delivery innovations adopted by social enterprises, including subscription-based primary healthcare, mobile medical units for remote areas, protocol-based, standardized care, and gender-inclusive healthcare services.

The case studies and analysis under this study present several approaches not widely covered in existing literature. For example, one enterprise developed a next-generation MRI scanner that is more affordable and accessible, designed to suit the average Indian physique and body size, reflecting the integration of technology and social impact. Another enterprise adopted standardization in healthcare through a technology platform.

The study demonstrates how enterprises adapt their models based on geographic location. It is seen that the social enterprises in big cities focus on scale and efficiency, whereas those in small towns emphasize accessibility and basic healthcare. This contrasts with the traditional literature, which focuses on direct service provision, employment creation, resource mobilization, and advocacy (Doherty et al., 2014).

The literature review highlights that "social enterprise requires entrepreneurial qualities with an emphasis on earned income" (Wendy Pardee, 2010). This is further supported by the study's findings, which reveal the adoption of several innovative approaches to mitigate operational and market risks. For operational risk management, the study shows that enterprises are adopting quality standardization protocols, integrating technology to improve efficiency, forging strategic partnerships, and pursuing phased market entry. For market risk management, enterprises are seen to have market validation through pilots, strategic partnerships, diversified service offerings and geographic expansion strategies.

The study identifies several risk management approaches used by social enterprises that are not widely covered in the existing literature, for example, location-based risk mitigation, in which the enterprise focuses on making MRI technology accessible in small and medium-sized towns and cities, as well as in remote areas. Another approach is technology integration, where the enterprise has built a technology platform through which they are standardizing the care that they are giving. A unique approach identified by the study and not widely covered in traditional literature is partnership-based risk sharing to share operational risks, access new markets, ensure quality standards, and build credibility. Traditional literature had mainly focused on the social enterprises adopting financial sustainability, market competition and operational efficiency for risk management (Austin et al., 2006).

In the context of financial risk management for social enterprises, the existing literature states that "the existence of such social enterprises without additional state and public support is impossible" (Akbulaev et al., 2019). This study goes into detail and reveals several innovative approaches, like funding diversification and revenue model innovation. The fund diversification strategies adopted by the social enterprises covered in the study include blended finance, commercial investments, government grants, and patient capital. Revenue model innovations identified by the study include subscription-based services, pay-as-you-use models, insurance integration into healthcare service delivery, and multiple revenue streams. The existing literature mainly deals with grant funding, donor relationships, and commercial revenue (Nicholls, 2009).

The literature review highlights that "social enterprises can deliver social impact through business models that use principles of circular economy" (Stratan, 2017). The study findings reveal several innovative approaches for achieving business viability by social enterprises. This includes improving operational efficiency through technology integration, standardized protocols, cost optimization, and quality management. In addition, the social enterprises are seen to ensure market expansion, including geographic expansion and service diversification, and to engage in partnership development and customer segment focus. While the existing literature on the business viability of social enterprises focuses on financial sustainability, social impact measurement, and stakeholder management, the study highlights the issues of technology-driven efficiency, location-based business model viability, and partnership-based growth.

In the context of social enterprises' business viability, the study examines the role of location, including strategies for big cities vs. small towns, adapting business models to local contexts, geographic expansion strategies, and location-specific partnerships. In terms of technology integration to enhance business viability, the study highlights digital platforms for healthcare delivery, technology-driven standardization, innovation in medical devices, and the adoption of telemedicine solutions. Going deeper into the financial innovations adopted by the studied healthcare social enterprises, it shows the leverage achieved through blended financing, subscription models, insurance integration, and multiple revenue streams.

These insights complement and extend existing literature, providing a more nuanced understanding of how social enterprises operate in practice. The theoretical implications of the study's findings include the need for location-specific theories, the integration of technology into social enterprise models, and the role of partnerships in risk management. The practical implications are the importance of context-specific strategies, the role of technology in scaling, the need for innovative financing and the importance of partnerships.

5.3. Risks Faced by Healthcare Social Enterprises

Social enterprises face unique risks and challenges, as discussed in the previous sections. Massarsky had mentioned that "an overwhelming percentage of social enterprise organizations (71%) are unprofitable and many fail within their first five years" (Massarsky, 2006). In terms of business risk, research by Bradach and Foster revealed that "social enterprise may lead to mission drift and less service delivered to the original recipients of services" (Bradach & Foster, 2005). Regarding financial risk, the literature states that "social enterprises face unique challenges in accessing capital and maintaining financial sustainability while pursuing their social mission" (Nicholls, 2009).

This study delves into the specifics of the business risks faced by healthcare social enterprises, highlighting operational, quality control, and human resource risks. The case studies reveal that operating mobile medical units and satellite centers in remote areas can pose logistical challenges for healthcare service provider enterprises. Also, attracting and retaining qualified medical professionals in remote areas can be difficult. Maintaining consistent quality across multiple services and satellite centers can be challenging for networked primary healthcare enterprises.

In terms of financial risks, the study shows that healthcare social enterprises are dependent on funding and have high leverage. There is a funding risk due to reliance on grants and recoverable grants. This is because grants are one-time funding, and there is no certainty of continued grant funding in the future. Added to this is the issue of a high leverage ratio, riding the cash infusion from grants.

The study also highlights location-specific risks that are not adequately dealt with by the existing literature on social enterprises. The case studies reveal that healthcare social enterprises in big cities face business risks, including higher operating costs, intense competition, quality expectations, and regulatory compliance. The financial challenges that these enterprises face in big cities include higher capital requirements, cost pressures, market competition and revenue uncertainties. On the other hand, healthcare enterprises in smaller towns face business risks such as a limited skilled workforce, infrastructure challenges, remote operations, and quality maintenance. They also face financial constraints arising from limited market size, resource constraints, high infrastructure costs, and working capital needs.

Other risks faced by social enterprises, as per the existing literature, include partnership risks. As per the literature,

"Partnership risks in social enterprises include mission alignment challenges, power imbalances, and operational coordination difficulties" (Austin & Seitanidi, 2012). The study's findings show that reliance on partnerships with government healthcare facilities may pose risks if these partnerships change or the rapport with government officials and political representatives shifts. The literature also discusses the risks of innovation and stakeholder engagement in the market for social enterprises. Santos et al (2015) mention, "Social enterprises face significant risks in technology adoption and innovation, particularly in resource-constrained environments". While Wendy Pardee (2010) says, "Social enterprises must navigate complex stakeholder relationships while maintaining their social mission," the study links technology adoption risk with market acceptance risk and shows that new technologies developed by social enterprises face market acceptance risk. There is a risk that hospitals and healthcare providers may be hesitant to adopt a new, unproven technology. The study also shows that innovations carry intellectual property (IP) risk. While the studied enterprises have filed patents, there is always a risk of IP infringement.

This comprehensive analysis demonstrates that social enterprises face complex business and financial risks that require careful management. The case studies provide insights that extend beyond existing literature, particularly in understanding location-specific risks, technology-related challenges, partnership complexities and implementation considerations. These insights contribute to both theory and practice by extending theoretical understanding, providing practical guidance, identifying success factors and highlighting implementation considerations.

5.4. *How Blended Finance Enables Healthcare Social Enterprises to Address Risks and Social Impact*

Blended finance has emerged as a critical tool for supporting social enterprises. It is a relatively new phenomenon. Blended finance was first mentioned as an option for financing development globally in the Addis Ababa Action Agenda, where it was defined as a mechanism "which combines concessional public finance with non-concessional private finance and expertise from the public and private sector" (UN, 2015). The consultation paper of the Blended Finance Task Force quoted the United Nations estimation of around "$6 trillion required annually to achieve the Sustainable Development Goals by 2030, with the gap being $2-3 trillion per year" (Taskforce, B.F., 2018). This ability of blended finance to mobilize additional resources is also borne out by the study's findings.

Regarding *SAMRIDH's* blended finance for healthcare in India, the study notes that blended finance mitigates financial risks by providing cash infusions from *SAMRIDH*. This initial funding helped mitigate early-stage financial risks by providing capital without immediate repayment pressure. The social enterprises studied were able to leverage 8-12 times the grants received from *the SAMRIDH* blended finance initiative.

The study offers new insights into the geographic specificity of differences in the use of blended finance by social enterprises. The study shows that healthcare social enterprises in big cities tend to use blended finance to leverage additional funding, support adherence to environmental considerations, and obtain patents and clearances. In contrast, those in small cities use blended finance to transition to profitability, build long-term capacity, expand markets, and grow revenue.

The current literature has extensively focused on the risk-mitigation role of blended finance. As per OECD (2018), "Blended finance can help de-risk investments and attract private capital to sustainable development projects", which is supported by the study. The study findings reveal the use of concessional capital by the healthcare social enterprises. The enterprises were able to get additional funding, and the additional cash infusion supported revenue growth. Literature review also found that blended finance can support operational improvements and capacity building (Sierra-Escalante & Karlin, 2021). This is borne out by the study, which found that *SAMRIDH* grants helped the enterprise strengthen its technical and sales teams, thereby addressing operational risks associated with scaling.

The adoption of blended finance by foundations and social organizations to enhance social impact is also mentioned in the literature. As noted in previous chapters, "some of the more forward-thinking foundations and social investors have realized that the current methods of financing social enterprises are inefficient, for the enterprises and themselves, and have started working to broaden the access to capital" (Bugg-Levine, et al, 2012). This is mirrored in the outreach services undertaken by the non-profit arm of the healthcare enterprise studied, where non-revenue-generating mobile units and satellite clinics, supported by concessional capital, increase access to healthcare by bringing health services directly to underserved hilly areas through telemedicine and MMUs. The concessional capital under the blended financing arrangement also supports ongoing innovation and product development, as well as the expansion of healthcare services in smaller towns, semi-urban areas, rural areas, and villages, as the study findings show.

The literature on the interplay of risk mitigation and impact enhancement in the role of blended finance shows that "as firms are stabilized and renewed but remain exposed to significant financial and operational risks, projects can still address critical issues of inclusion, gender equality, and climate sustainability" (Sierra-Escalante & Karlin, 2021). The study on healthcare social enterprises in

India brings several new insights to support this. This study highlights the diverse uses of blended finance by social enterprises,

tailored to different contexts. These contexts include urban versus rural applications, scale-up versus basic service support and technology versus infrastructure focus. The study also highlights different implementation strategies enabled by blended finance and associated technical assistance. These include context-specific approaches, partnership development, risk management and impact measurement. The study shows that blended finance supports innovation among social enterprises by funding R&D, product development, service innovation, and digital transformation. The study also highlights the implementation support provided by blended finance in terms of technology adoption, system integration, capacity building and quality enhancement.

Thus, we see that the study highlights the financing as well as organizational development role played by blended finance, combining funding and technical assistance aspects. This is in addition to the risk mitigation and financing roles of blended finance, which are addressed by the existing body of literature on social enterprises and blended finance. The study shows how blended finance supports capacity building, helps forge strategic partnerships, facilitates regulatory and environmental compliance, and tests market feasibility for new product and service innovations. Thus, the study presents a comprehensive model for the application of blended finance, not widely covered in the existing literature.

Chapter 6 | Summary, Implications, and Recommendations

6.1. Summary

While industries focus primarily on economic impact, with social and environmental impact as an additionality to their economic activity, non-profits focus primarily on social and/or environmental impact, with economic impact as an additionality. It is only the social enterprises that focus on all three aspects of the triple bottom line as their primary focus. Also, social enterprises get blended funding, which is a mix of commercial investment and philanthropic/public funding, whereas industries get commercial investments, which is showing an ESG lens of investing lately. On the other hand, non-profits receive only philanthropic and public funding, with no commercial investments, as their activities are essentially non-commercial.

Currently, there is a research gap in a comprehensive blended financing framework to evaluate commercial, philanthropic, and public investments in SEs. The ESG framework, which guides commercial investments into sustainable businesses, does not mention the de-risking role of pubic and philanthropic funds in a blended financing scenario. On the other hand, the blended finance literature discusses the de-risking role of public and philanthropic funds in attracting commercial investment. However, it overlooks how these non-commercial investment decisions are made and how funders reconcile economic, environmental, and social priorities and expenditures. The literature is also silent on any common or mutually supportive investment decision-making tool guiding commercial, philanthropic, and public funding of SEs. There is also a very specific research gap on healthcare SEs, which has become important in the post-COVID pandemic world.

In this context, this research adopts a qualitative approach to develop a conceptual model of how blended finance addresses the business and financial risks faced by healthcare social enterprises in their quest for economic sustainability and social impact. The method relies on framework analysis and grounded theory analysis using content and narrative analysis of the in-depth interviews and document reviews used. Finally, a conceptual framework is suggested linking blended finance and social enterprises to sustainable development outcomes.

The four case studies show that each enterprise has developed innovative approaches to address healthcare challenges. Whether through technology (MRI and ECG devices), service delivery (subscription-based primary care), or hybrid models (hospital with outreach services), innovation is central to their success. The study's findings also suggest that blended finance is emerging as a crucial enabler for healthcare social enterprises. It helps mitigate early-stage risks, attract commercial capital, support innovation and R&D, enable market expansion, and maintain affordability while building financial sustainability.

The study reveals significant differences between enterprises in big cities and those in small towns. The social enterprises located in bigger cities have better access to funding and resources, a more competitive environment, a larger potential market and higher operating costs. In contrast, the enterprises in smaller towns have a greater focus on basic healthcare needs, a more challenging operating environment, stronger community connections and lower operating costs.

The study shows that social enterprises address social impact, business risks, financial risks, and business viability through innovative approaches that go beyond traditional understanding. The case studies hint at the importance of the context in which social enterprises operate in shaping social enterprise strategies, the crucial role of technology in enabling scale and efficiency, the significance of partnerships in risk management, and the innovation in financial models, particularly blended finance.

The study highlights the role of blended finance in mitigating the risks faced by social enterprises and enhancing social impact, particularly for the four types of healthcare social enterprises studied in India. It indicates that blended finance mitigates the risks faced by healthcare social enterprises through financial risk reduction, operational risk management, and market risk mitigation. Regarding social impact, the study shows that blended finance helps social enterprises address it by improving access, enhancing quality, achieving scale, and supporting innovation.

While the existing literature discusses the risk-mitigation role of blended finance in the context of social enterprises and technical assistance as enabling access to capital, this study highlights the importance of blended finance in nurturing and supporting enterprises. The study shows how blended finance supports capacity building, helps forge strategic partnerships, facilitates regulatory and environmental compliance, and tests market feasibility for new product and service innovations. Thus, the study presents a comprehensive model of the application of blended finance that has not been dealt with in the existing literature.

6.2. Implications

The study brings out several implications for policy and practice. There is a need for expanded blended finance mechanisms. It is important to have tailored support based on enterprise type and location. The role of technology in enabling new healthcare delivery models has also been highlighted through these case studies. All these need building ecosystems that support social enterprises. These insights can inform the development of more effective support mechanisms for social enterprises in general and healthcare social enterprises in particular, ultimately contributing to improved triple bottom line of environmental, social and economic sustainability in the context of low- and middle-income countries like India.

This study demonstrates that blended finance plays a crucial role in enabling social enterprises to address both risks and social impact objectives, and provides valuable insights that extend beyond existing literature, particularly in understanding the specific context of healthcare social enterprises and the success factors. It highlights the significance of location considerations, market conditions, resource availability, and partnership opportunities. This is presented alongside success factors such as strong partnerships, technology integration, quality focus, and impact measurement.

For social enterprises, this implies developing comprehensive blended finance strategies, focusing on location-specific approaches, integrating technology into their business processes, and building strong partnerships. For policymakers, this implies creating enabling environments, supporting innovation, facilitating partnerships, and enabling market development. For investors using blended finance to support social enterprises, the implications are understanding local contexts, supporting technology integration, enabling innovative financing, and focusing on long-term sustainability.

To conclude, the study implies the need to shift away from viewing blended finance purely as a financing tool and risk-mitigation enabler for social enterprises. The investors and policymakers need to consider blended finance as a holistic strategy that involves long-term support for social enterprises, including forging strategic partnerships, facilitating regulatory and environmental compliance, enabling market expansion into difficult-to-reach areas and populations, and fostering innovation and technology adoption.

6.3. Recommendations for Future Research

Given the limited number of healthcare social enterprises adopting blended finance in the Indian context, more research is needed with a larger sample of social enterprises and a broader range of blended finance structures to further test the suggested framework for how blended finance enables social enterprises to address risks and impact.

Future research also needs to explore context-specific strategies, technology integration, partnership models and financial innovations for social enterprises adopting blended finance. These aspects were hinted at in this study but need deeper treatment in future research. Other areas of deeper enquiry include risk management approaches, success factors, performance metrics and impact measurement of social enterprises and their use of blended finance as an enabler.

In the future, more practical research and implementation studies can include best practices, success factors, ways to mitigate challenges, and methods for performance improvement. Impact studies can include measuring risk management effectiveness, strategy success, performance measurement, and social impact assessment for social enterprises engaged in the social sector, producing social and merit goods such as health.

While this research suggests a framework for healthcare social enterprises using blended finance to address risks and social impact, future research can test whether blended finance actually reduces risks and increases social implications. Also, future research can test the framework suggested here to see whether it applies to other social sectors, such as education, nutrition, livelihoods, water and sanitation, and care for the disabled, the old, and children.

Nonetheless, the framework suggested in this research is a step towards answering crucial financial structuring questions that global investors may have while looking for investment opportunities in sustainable development enterprises.

6.4. Conclusion

The study shows that social enterprises address social impact, business risks, financial risks, and business viability through innovative approaches that go beyond traditional understanding. The case studies hint at the importance of context in shaping social enterprise strategies, the crucial role of technology in enabling scale and efficiency, the significance of partnerships in risk management and the innovation in financial models, particularly blended finance.

The study highlights the role of blended finance in mitigating the risks faced by social enterprises and enhancing social impact, particularly among the four types of healthcare social enterprises studied in India. It indicates that blended finance mitigates the risks faced by healthcare social enterprises through financial risk reduction, operational risk management, and market risk mitigation. On social impact, the study shows that blended finance helps social enterprises address it by improving access, enhancing quality, achieving scale, and supporting innovation.

The study hints at a need for expanded blended finance mechanisms. It is important to have tailored support based on enterprise type and location. The role of technology in enabling new healthcare delivery models has also been highlighted through these case studies. All these need building ecosystems that support social enterprises. These insights can inform the development of more effective support mechanisms for social enterprises in general and healthcare social enterprises in particular, ultimately contributing to improved triple bottom line of environmental, social and economic sustainability in the context of low- and middle-income countries like India.

This implies that there is a need to stop viewing blended finance solely as a financing tool and risk-mitigation enabler for social enterprises. Instead, investors and policymakers need to consider blended finance as a holistic strategy that provides long-term support to social enterprises by forging strategic partnerships, facilitating regulatory and environmental compliance, enabling market expansion into difficult-to-reach areas and populations, and fostering innovation and technology adoption.

Given the limited number of healthcare social enterprises adopting blended finance in the Indian context, more research is needed with a larger sample of social enterprises and a broader range of blended finance structures to further test the suggested framework for how blended finance enables social enterprises to address risks and impact. Nonetheless, the conceptual model suggested in this research is a step towards answering crucial financial structuring questions that global investors may have while looking for investment opportunities in sustainable development enterprises.

Appendices

Appendix A: Informed Consent

The following template was used to obtain informed consent from the four entrepreneurs interviewed for the four case studies.

> Hello, I am Gautam Chakraborty, a student in the Global Doctorate in Business Administration at the Swiss School of Business and Management, Geneva.
>
> This interview is conducted as part of my doctoral program on the topic of blended finance in the context of healthcare social enterprises in India. I am especially interested in your journey and experiences of starting and growing your business while balancing financial viability and social/health impact.
>
> If it is okay with you, I will be tape recording our conversation. The purpose is to get all the details while also being able to carry on an attentive conversation with you. I assure you that all your comments will remain confidential. I will compile a report containing all comments and responses without any references to individuals.
>
> Do I have your consent?

Appendix B: Interview Guide

If consent is given, start recording and reconfirm the consent for recording purposes, using the checklist below. If consent is not given, do not proceed with the interview.

Checklist:

1. Why did you start the business? (probe the impact versus profit motivation)
2. How did you start the journey so far? (probe the economic viability and impact story)
3. How do you finance the business?
4. How do you finance the impact?
5. Experience with blended finance (probe the contribution to cash flow, profitability, impact, and scale)
6. What are the business (revenue) and financial (capital mix) risks that you face?
7. What support do you need to address those business and financial risks?
8. What support do you need for sustaining and scaling the impact?

Appendix C: Abbreviations

AUM	Assets Under Management
B2B	Business to Business
B2C	Business to Customer
BCG	Boston Consulting Group
CDCs	Community Development Corporations
CDSCO	Central Drugs Control Organization of India
CEc	Capital Stock of the Economy
CEn	Capital Stock of the Environment
CEO	Chief Executive Officer
CGHS	Central Government Health Service
CHC	Community Health Center
COVID-19	Coronavirus Disease 2019
CS	Capital Stock of the Society
CSD	Capital Stock of Sustainable Development
CSR	Corporate Social Responsibility
CT	Computed Tomography Scan
DFC	US Government's Development Finance Corporation
DFI	Development Finance Institutions
EBIDTA	Earnings Before Interest, Taxes, Depreciation, and Amortization
ECG	Electrocardiogram
ECHS	Employees Contributory Health Scheme
ERCP	Endoscopic Retrograde Cholangiopancreatography
ESG	Environment-Social-Governance Lensed Investments
ESI	Employees State Insurance
GMP	Good Manufacturing Practices
HDU	High Dependency Unit
ICU	Intensive Care Unit
IDI	In-depth Interview
IFC	International Finance Corporation
IITD	Indian Institute of Technology, Delhi
IP	Intellectual Property
ISE	International Securities Exchange
IUCN	International Union for the Conservation of Nature
MAIN	Mind, Artefact, Institution and Nature

MBBS	Bachelor of Medicine and Bachelor of Surgery
MMU	Mobile Medical Unit
MONET	Monitoring of Sustainable Development Project
MRI	Magnetic Resonance Imaging
NABH	National Accreditation Board for Hospitals
NGO	Non-Government Organizations
NICU	Newborn Intensive Care Unit
NITI	National Institution for Transforming India
OECD	Organization of Economic Co-operation and Development
OPD	Out-Patient Department
PHC	Primary Health Center
R&D	Research and Development
SDGs	Sustainable Development Goals
SDG-3	Sustainable Development Goal-3 (good health and well-being)
SDG-4	Sustainable Development Goal-4 (quality education)
SDG-5	Sustainable Development Goal-5 (gender equality)
SDG-8	Sustainable Development Goal-8 (decent work and economic growth)
SDG-9	Sustainable Development Goal-9 (industry, innovation, and infrastructure)
SDG-10	Sustainable Development Goal-10 (reduced inequalities)
SEs	Social Enterprises
SMEs	Small and Medium Enterprises
TBL	Triple Bottom Line
TPA	Third Party Administrator
TSU	Technical Support Unit
UN	United Nations
USAID	United States Agency for International Development
WCED	World Commission on Environment and Development
WHO	World Health Organization

Appendix D: Definition of Terms

Access to Capital	The ability of individuals and businesses to obtain financial services, such as loans, deposits, insurance, and payment facilities.
Accessibility	All people, regardless of ability, can obtain the goods, services or information offered by a provider.
Affirmative Action	A set of policies and procedures that are intended to eliminate discrimination and improve opportunities for underrepresented groups in healthcare, education, livelihood and other social services.
Affordability	A condition of goods or services being low-priced enough for people across all socio-economic groups to be able to obtain them.
Blended Finance	Use of philanthropic and public concessional capital to attract private and institutional investment for achieving social and development impact, while at the same time ensuring economic viability of the activity or business.
Business Advisory	A professional service that provides strategic guidance and advice to help businesses achieve their goals and manage risks.
Business Level Blended Finance	Mixing philanthropic and public concessional capital with the commercial long-term and short-term liabilities of a business entity to reduce risk and increase economic, social and environmental impact.
Business Model	An economic entity's operational and financial sustainability plan, including identifying revenue sources, customer base, products and services offered, and details of financing.
Business Risk	An enterprise's business risk is related to its ability to generate enough revenue to cover its operating expenses and turn a profit. Business risk can be caused by internal and external factors, such as ineffective management, reputational risk, or industry-specific risks.
Capital Investment	The act of investing money in a company to help it grow or increase productivity, usually long-term and aimed at acquiring assets with a life cycle of at least one year.
Conceptual Modeling	The process of creating a high-level representation of a system or concept to make it easier to understand, and

	can be used to represent physical or social concepts.
Concessional Capital	A type of financing that offers more favorable terms than the market, such as zero or lower interest rates, non-returnable or with longer repayment periods, or partial guarantees and is often used to fund projects that have a high social, environmental, or developmental impact, but may not be commercially viable.
Credit Enhancement	It is a strategy that improves a business's credit risk profile to help it secure better terms for repaying debt, primarily by rejigging its liabilities and assets on the balance sheet.
De-risking	The phenomenon of financial institutions terminating or restricting business relationships with risky clients. It is reducing the risk of investment by pulling out of a risky investment.
Development Impact/Outcome	The effect of a business or a program on the target population, especially in terms of achieving sustainable development goals that are people-centered.
Economic Impact	A financial effect that something, especially something new, has on a situation or person.
Environmental Impact	Changes in the natural or built environment resulting directly from an activity that can have adverse effects on air, land, water, fish, wildlife, or the inhabitants of the ecosystem.
Environment-Social-Governance (ESG)	It is a framework comprising the three pillars of environmental impact, social impact and corporate governance that companies are expected to report on to capture all the non-financial risks and opportunities inherent to a company's day-to-day activities.
Fee-for-service Model	The fee-for-service model of social enterprise commercializes its social services and then sells them directly to the target populations or clients. This involves a payment structure where the service provider receives payment for each service they deliver.
Financial Advisory	Financial advisory is financial advice or guidance provided to a business entity. It involves assistance with preparing investment pitches, capital mix options, investment management and tax planning.
Financial Risk	A company's financial risk is related to its ability to manage its debt and financial leverage. This includes the risk of defaulting on debt payments. Financial risk

	can be caused by external factors, such as market movements (inflation, interest rates, and foreign exchange rates), or by internal financing factors (debt-equity ratio, net working capital ratio, reserves, and surpluses).
Financing Model	A capital mix arrangement that is opted for to meet the anticipated short-term and long-term financial requirements of a business.
Framework Analysis	A systematic method used in qualitative research to analyze data by organizing it into a structured framework, typically consisting of categories and themes.
Fund	Pooled capital of investors that enables the fund manager to make investment decisions on their (the investors) behalf.
Funding Facility	A formal financial assistance program by one or a group of financiers to help companies that require operating capital, for a specific purpose.
Grounded Theory Analysis	Grounded theory analysis, also known as constant comparative analysis or theoretical sampling, is an inductive approach in which researchers use data to develop a new theory.
Health Outcomes	Health outcomes are the health consequences that result from the planned treatment, intervention, or series of interventions within the healthcare system. Health outcomes may be calculated for an individual, group, or population.
In-depth Interview	A qualitative research method that involves having a detailed conversation with an individual or a small group of people to learn about their perspectives on a topic. It is an open-ended, discovery-oriented method to obtain detailed information about a topic from a stakeholder.
Information Asymmetry	Simply put, it is a situation where one party has more or better information than another. In healthcare, doctors typically know much more about treatment options and procedures, potentially leaving patients struggling to make informed decisions about their care. This may lead to over-prescription and irrational diagnostics, and the patient has to depend on what the doctor says.
Initial Working Capital	The amount of money a business needs at the initial stage to start or grow, before the revenue stream can fully sustain the costs.

Interest Subvention	A grant made to lower the interest payment burden of borrowers in a certain situation, like a natural disaster, economy-wide stress, or certain priority businesses that are socially relevant but need a subsidy to have a more viable capital structure.
Market Failure	It is an economic situation defined by an inefficient distribution of goods and services. In healthcare, due to information asymmetry and supplier-induced demand, the market fails to determine the true price and optimal supply of goods and services to the needy.
Merit Goods	Merit goods have characteristics of both private goods and public goods. Its consumption by an individual confers a benefit on that individual, like a private good, but it is also beneficial to the society in which the individual lives, like a public good. Immunization and preventive, primary healthcare are examples of merit goods.
Narrative Analysis	A narrative analysis is a qualitative research method based on analyzing the human experience of a phenomenon or process, in the form of a story or narrative.
Partnership Arrangement for Financing	It is a formal arrangement between two or more individuals or organizations in which each party agrees to share financial resources on a mutually agreed theme or cause, while maintaining complete control over the decision-making and process for contributing their respective shares of the funds. There is pooling of intent and action, but no pooling of funds.
Pay-as-you-use Model	It is a pricing model in which customers are charged based on the use of a commodity or equipment, rather than the full cost upfront.
Physical Environment	It includes the natural environment in which human society lives, including land, air, water, flora, fauna and natural resources.
Phlebotomists	Medical professionals/technicians who collect blood from patients and prepare the samples for testing
Portfolio-level Blended Finance	This involves blending concessional capital with commercial investment at an aggregate "fund" level to address portfolio-level risks and impacts. It is structuring concessional capital to address the aggregated risks and impacts of an investment portfolio, thereby lowering the risk of commercial

	investments in the portfolio businesses.
Qualitative Case Study	It involves a deep dive into a phenomenon or object of research, using data from in-depth interviews, observations, and documents.
Seed Funding	It is the early-stage capital required to kick-start the development of a new enterprise or startup.
Shark Tank (India)	Shark Tank (India) is a television show where aspiring entrepreneurs pitch their emerging business ideas to a panel of successful investors, known as "sharks." The "sharks" decide whether to invest their own money in exchange for a stake in the company.
Social Goods	Social goods are products and services that benefit the community as a whole. They are also known as public goods or common goods. Examples of social goods include clean air, clean water, healthcare, and education.
Social Enterprises	These are businesses that take a commercial approach to deliver environmental and social goods and services while maintaining the business's financial and commercial viability. "Social Enterprise" and "social business" are used interchangeably in this research.
Social Environment	It comprises people and institutions that serve the social purposes of health, well-being, and the development of the people who constitute the society.
Social Impact	Effects on people and communities, such as job creation, improved education and health, cultural preservation, etc.
Subscription-based Model	It is a recurring revenue model in which customers pay a recurring, uniform fee to avail a defined package of services or goods.
Supplier-induced Demand	It is a phenomenon in which a provider of a product or service stimulates or creates greater demand for their offering than would otherwise exist in the market.
Sustainable Development Goals (SDGs)	These are 17 goals adopted by the United Nations' member states in 2015 to protect the planet while achieving prosperity for people. The goals span environmental preservation, poverty reduction, and improved education and health.
Technical Assistance (TA)	This includes non-monetary assistance, comprising a mix of advisory services for targeted organizations to help them achieve their goals while addressing knowledge, expertise, and resource gaps.

Triple Bottom Line (TBL)	This is a conceptual framework of development that addresses the needs of the planet, people and profits simultaneously in a win-win manner for all.
White Category Company	The Central Pollution Control Board (CPCB) of India classifies industries into white, red, orange, and green categories based on their pollution index. Industries with a pollution index of less than 20 are classified as white-category industries, which are considered environmentally non-polluting.
Working Capital Financing	Financing, mostly short-term, to cover day-to-day business operations.

References

1. Akbulaev, N., Aliyev, Y. and Ahmadov, T. (2019). Research Models for Financing Social Business: Theory and Practice. *Heliyon, 5*(5), e01599.
2. Alter, K. (2007). Social Enterprise Typology. Virtue Ventures LLC, 12(1), pp.1-124.
3. Anas Ali Al-Qudah, M., Manaf Al-Okaily and Hamza Alqudah (2022). The relationship between social entrepreneurship and sustainable development from an economic growth perspective: 15 'RCEP' countries. *Journal of Sustainable Finance and Investment,* 12(1), 44-61.
4. Armstrong, A. (2020). Ethics and ESG. Australasian Accounting. *Business and Finance Journal,* 14(3), 6-17.
5. Austin, J., Stevenson, H. and Wei–Skillern, J. (2006). Social and commercial entrepreneurship: same, different, or both? *Entrepreneurship Theory and Practice,* 30(1), 1-22.
6. Austin, J.E. and Seitanidi, M.M. (2012). Collaborative value creation: A review of partnering between non-profits and businesses: Part I. Value creation spectrum and collaboration stages. *Non-profit and Voluntary Sector Quarterly,* 41(5), 726-758.
7. Banks, J.A. (1972). *The Sociology of Social Movements* (p. 17). London: Macmillan.
8. Basile, I. and Dutra, J. (2019). *Blended Finance Funds and Facilities: 2018 Survey Results,* OECD Development Co-operation Working Papers, No. 59, OECD Publishing, Paris.

9. Bataeva, B.S. (2015). The approaches to social entrepreneurship in Russia and abroad. *Entrepreneurship and Business in the Conditions of Economic Instability*, pp. 221-223.
10. Baxter, P. and Jack, S. (2008). Qualitative case study methodology: Study design and implementation for novice researchers. *The Qualitative Report*, 13, 544–559.
11. Beal, D., Eccles, R., Hansell, G., Lesser, R., Unnikrishnan, S., Woods, W. and Young, D. (2017). *Total societal impact: A new lens for strategy*. BCG: Boston, MA, USA.
12. Bertolotti, A. (2020). Effectively managing risks in an ESG portfolio. *Journal of Risk Management in Financial Institutions*, 13(3), 202-211.
13. Bhattacharya, D. and Khan, S.S. (2018). *Is blended finance trending in LDCs? Perspectives from the ground.* Southern Voice Occasional Paper, No.49.
14. Bornstein, D. (2007). *How to change the world – social entrepreneurs and the power of new ideas*. Oxford University Press.
15. Borzaga, C. and Depedri, S. (2014). Co-operatives Providing Welfare Services: The Case of Italian Social Co-operatives. In *Co-operative Innovations in China and the West* (pp. 126-142). Palgrave Macmillan.
16. Bossel, H. (1999). *Indicators for sustainable development: theory, method, applications* (p. 138). IISD, Winnipeg.
17. Bowen, H.R. (2013). *Social Responsibilities of the Businessman*. University of Iowa Press.
18. Broadstock, D.C., Chan, K., Cheng, L.T. and Wang, X. (2021). The role of ESG performance during times of financial crisis: Evidence from COVID-19 in China. *Finance Research Letters*, 38, 101716.
19. Bugg-Levine, A., Kogut, B. and Kulatilaka, N. (2012). A new approach to funding social enterprises. *Harvard Business Review*, 90(1/2), 118-123.

20. Carlson, C., Cutcher-Gershenfeld, J. and Kriegsman, M. (Eds.) (2024). *The Heller Social Impact Case Collection: Reimagining Capitalism Through Case-based Learning*. Brandeis University Press.
21. Chakraborty, G. and Rao, N. (2022). Attaining Sustainable Development Outcomes Through Blended Financing of Social Enterprises. *Global Journal of Business and Integral Security.*
22. Christoforou, A. and Davis, J.B. (2014). Social Capital: Social Values, Power, and Social Identity. In *Social Capital and Economics* (pp. 25-34). Routledge.
23. Dalal, K.K. and Thaker, N. (2019). ESG and corporate financial performance: A panel study of Indian companies. *IUP Journal of Corporate Governance*, 18(1), 44-59.
24. Dan, C. D., Luminita, M.G., Alin, A., & Vasile, D. (2015). The Components of Sustainable Development – A Possible Approach. *Procedia Economics and Finance*, 26, 806-811.
25. Dempsey, N., Bramley, G., Power, S. and Brown, C. (2011). The social dimension. *Sustainable Development*, 19(5), 289-300.
26. Doherty, B., Haugh, H. and Lyon, F. (2014). Social enterprises as hybrid organizations. *International Journal of Management Reviews*, 16(4), 417-436.
27. Drayton, W., Brown, C. and Hillhouse, K. (2006). Integrating social entrepreneurs into the 'health for all' formula. *WHO Bulletin*, 84, 591.
28. Duran, D.C., Gogan, L.M., Artene, A. and Duran, V. (2015). The components of sustainable development: a possible approach. *Procedia Economics and Finance*, 26, 806-811.
29. Eden, S.E. (1994). Using sustainable development: The business case. *Global Environmental Change*, 4(2), 160-167.
30. Ekren, D.C. and Şentürk, T. (2021). How Can Social Marketing and Social Enterprises Promote Sustainable Development. *Journal of International Social Research*, 14(77), 1280-1294.

31. Elkington, J. (1997). *The triple bottom line*. Environmental management: Readings and cases, 2, 49-66.

32. Elkington, J. (2018). "25 years ago, I coined the phrase 'triple bottom line'. *Harvard Business Review*, 25, 2-5.

33. Emerson, J. and Twersky, F. (Eds.) (1996). *New Social Entrepreneurs…* Roberts Foundation.

34. Eskandarpour, M., Dejax, P., Miemczyk, J. & Péton, O. (2015). Sustainable supply chain network design. *Omega*, 54, 11-32.

35. Fatemi, A., Glaum, M. & Kaiser, S. (2018). ESG performance and firm value. *Global Finance Journal*, 38, 45-64.

36. Foster, W. and Bradach, J. (2005). Should non-profits seek profits? *Harvard Business Review*, 83(2), 92-100.

37. Foubert, A.L. (2020). *ESG data integration by asset managers…*, Opimas.

38. Frant, F. and Minica, M. (2008). "The dimensions of durable development". *Annals of the University of Craiova*, 7(36).

39. Ghosh, S. and Rajan, J. (2019). The business case for SDGs. *International Journal of Sustainable Development and World Ecology*, 26(4), 344-353.

40. Gladwin, T.N., Kennelly, J.J. and Krause, T.S. (1995). Shifting paradigms. *Academy of Management Review*, 20(4), 874-907.

41. Goel, P. (2010). Triple Bottom Line Reporting. *Journal of Finance, Accounting and Management*, 1(1).

42. Gordon, K., Wilson, J., Tonner, A. and Shaw, E. (2018). How can social enterprises impact health. *International Journal of Entrepreneurial Behavior & Research*, 24(3), 697-713.

43. Gordon, K.… (2018). The Role of Socially Driven Community Food Projects. *BSA Annual Conference.*

44. Guijt, I. and Moiseev, A. (2001). *Resource kit for sustainability assessment*. IUCN.

45. Halinen, A. and Tornroos, J.A. (2005). Using case methods. *Journal of Business Research*, 58, 1285-1297.

46. Havemann, T., Negra, C. and Werneck, F. (2020). Blended finance for agriculture. *Agriculture and Human Values*, 37(4), 1281-1292.

47. Henderson, F., Steiner, A., et al. (2020). Social Enterprises' Impact on Older People's Health. *Health Promotion International*, 35(5), 1074-1084.

48. Ho, V.H. and Park, S.K. (2019). ESG Disclosure in Comparative Perspective. *UPenn JIL*, 41, 249.

49. Holt, D. and Littlewood, D. (2015). Identifying, mapping. *California Management Review*, 57(3), 107-125.

50. Jarvensivu, T. and Tornroos, J.A. (2010). Case study research. *Industrial Marketing Management*, 39, 100-108.

51. Kaarbo, J. & Beasley, R.K. (1999). A practical guide. *Political Psychology*, 20, 369-391.

52. Kassim, E.S. and Habib, M.M. (2020). Social Enterprise and Creation of Social Value Chain. *IJSCM*, 9(2), 205-210.

53. Keiner, M. (2005). *History, definition(s) and models of sustainable development*. ETH Zurich.

54. Khanna, T. (2018). *Trust: Creating the foundation for entrepreneurship in developing countries*. Berrett-Koehler.

55. Kharas, H., Prizzon, A. and Rogerson, A. (2014). *Financing the post-2015 SDGs*. ODI, London.

56. Kiiza, J., Nassimbwa, J. and Mulumba, M. (2019). Uganda. *Tanzania Journal of Development Studies*, 17(1), 42-65.

57. Kilgore-Nolan, M. (2021). The Ecosystem of Women's Health Social Enterprises. In *Entrepreneurship for Social Change*. Emerald.

58. Krajnc, D. and Glavič, P. (2005). A model for integrated assessment. *Resources, Conservation and Recycling*, 43(2), 189-208.

59. Leadbeater, C. (1997). *The rise of the social entrepreneur*. Demos.

60. Lokuwaduge, C.S.D.S. & Heenetigala, K. (2017). Integrating ESG disclosure. *Business Strategy and the Environment*, 26(4), 438-450.

61. Lopez-de-Silanes, F., McCahery, J.A. & Pudschedl, P.C. (2020). ESG performance and disclosure. *Singapore JLS*, 217-241.

62. Loviscek, V. (2021). Triple Bottom Line toward a holistic framework. *Revista de Administração Contemporânea*, 25(3), e200017.

63. Macassa, G. (2021). Social Enterprise, Population Health and SDG 3. *Annals of Global Health*, 87(1):52.

64. Martin, M. (2015). Building Impact Businesses through Hybrid Financing. *Entrepreneurship Research Journal*, 5, 109-126.

65. Massarsky, C.W. (2006). Coming of Age. *Research on Social Entrepreneurship*, 1, 67-88.

66. Mervelskemper, L. & Streit, D. (2017). Enhancing market valuation of ESG. *Business Strategy and the Environment*, 26(4), 536-549.

67. Milne, M.J. & Gray, R. (2013). W(h)ither ecology? *Journal of Business Ethics*, 118(1), 13-29.

68. Montabon, F., Pagell, M. & Wu, Z. (2016). Making sustainability sustainable. *JSCM*, 52(2), 11-27.

69. Moyo, D. (2010). *Dead Aid: Why Aid Is Not Working....* Penguin Books.

70. Nicholls, A. (2009). We do good things, don't we? *Accounting, Organizations and Society*, 34(6-7), 755-769.

71. NITI Aayog (2022). *Reimagining Healthcare in India through Blended Finance.*

72. Nyssens, M. (2006). *Social Enterprise.* EMES.

73. OECD (2015). *Blended Finance Vol. 1....* WEF.

74. OECD (2018). *OECD DAC Blended Finance Principles....*

75. Pardee, W. (2010). Effects of social enterprise among non-profit behavioral healthcare providers. Indiana University of Pennsylvania.

76. Pardee, W. (2010). *Effects of Social Enterprise among Non-profit Behavioral Healthcare Providers...* (duplicate).
77. Peattie, K. & Peattie, S. (2009). Social Marketing: A Pathway to Consumption Reduction? *JBR*, 62(2), 260-268.
78. Rahdari, A., Sepasi, S. & Moradi, M. (2016). Achieving sustainability through Schumpeterian. *JCP*, 137, 347-360.
79. Rashid, Y., et al. (2019). Case study method. *IJQM*, 18.
80. Roy, M.J., Donaldson, C., Baker, R. & Kerr, S. (2014). The Potential of Social Enterprise. *SSM*, 123, 182-193.
81. Rychetnik, L., et al. (2002). Criteria for Evaluating Evidence. *JECH*, 56(2), 119-127.
82. Santos, F., Pache, A.C. & Birkholz, C. (2015). Making hybrids work. *California Management Review*, 57(3), 36-58.
83. Scheyvens, R., Banks, G. & Hughes, E. (2016). The private sector and the SDGs. *Sustainable Development*, 24(6), 371-382.
84. Schleich, M.V. (2021). *Do ESG metrics impact financial performance in Brazil?* (Doctoral dissertation).
85. Sealey, K., Boschee, J., Emerson, J. & Sealey, W. (2000). *A Reader in Social Enterprise.*
86. Seelos, C. & Mair, J. (2005). Social entrepreneurship. *Business Horizons*, 48(3), 241-246.
87. Sierra-Escalante, K. & Karlin, A. (2021). *Blended Concessional Finance and COVID-19.*
88. Singh, A.P. & Rahman, Z. (2021). Integrating corporate sustainability and SDGs. *Cogent Business and Management*, 8(1).
89. Soukhasing, D., Dea, V. & Ruslim, C. (2017). Social finance and social enterprises. *JPP*, 1(3), 240-255.
90. Spangenberg, J.H. & Bonniot, O. (1998). *Sustainability indicators...* Wuppertal Papers.
91. Stenberg, J. (2001). *Bridging gaps: Sustainable development and local democracy processes.*
92. Stratan, D. (2017). Success factors of sustainable social enterprises. *VJBSD*, 6(1), 17-23.

93. Svensson, G., et al. (2016). A triple bottom line dominant logic. *JBBM*, 23(2), 153-188.
94. Taskforce, B.F. (2018). *Better Finance, Better World.*
95. Terziev, V. and Arabska, E. (2017). Social entrepreneurship. *IJRMEC*, 7(4), 41-46.
96. The Global Compact (2004). *Who cares wins....* UN.
97. UN (2000). United Nations Millennium Declaration.
98. UN (2015). *Addis Ababa Action Agenda...*
99. UN (2015). *Transforming Our World: The 2030 Agenda...*
100. USAID (2019). *Greater than the Sum of its Parts...* USAID.
101. Valentin, A. & Spangenberg, J.H. (1999). Indicators for sustainable communities. International Workshop.
102. Walker, H., Seuring, S., Sarkis, J. & Klassen, R. (2014). Sustainable operations management. *IJOPM*, 34(5).
103. Wall, G. & Gong, M. (2001). On exergy and sustainable development. *Exergy*, 1(3), 128-145.
104. WCED (1987). *Our common future.*
105. Williams, A. (2015). Aligning with the SDGs. *WBCSD & EMAN Symposium Proceedings*, 116-117.
106. Winter, M. & Knemeyer, A.M. (2013). Exploring the integration of sustainability. *IJPDLM*, 43(1), 18-38.
107. Zhan, J.X., Santos-Paulino, A.U. (2021). Investing in the SDGs. *JIBP*, 4, 166-183.
108. Zhang, D.D. & Swanson, L.A. (2014). Linking social entrepreneurship and sustainability. *Journal of Social Entrepreneurship*, 5(2), 175-191.
109. Ziolo, M., Bak, I., & Cheba, K. (2021). The role of sustainable finance. *TEDE*, 27(1), 45-70.